THE SHEIKH
OF
BAGHDAD

to Burgie
all the Best & enjoy
this Book

the Shiekh
Admiral

8-2-05

THE SHEIKH
OF
BAGHDAD

Tales of Celebrity and Terror
from Pro Wrestling's General Adnan

Adnan Alkaissy
with Ross Bernstein

TRIUMPH
B O O K S
CHICAGO

Library of Congress Cataloging-in-Publication Data

Alkaissy, Adnan, 1939–
    The Sheikh of Baghdad : tales of celebrity and terror from pro wrestling's General Adnan / Adnan Alkaissy with Ross Bernstein.
        p. cm.
    ISBN-13: 978-1-57243-730-2
    ISBN-10: 1-57243-730-8
        1. Alkaissy, Adnan, 1939– 2. Wrestlers—United States—Biography.
    3. Wrestlers—Iraq—Biography. I. Bernstein, Ross, 1969– II. Title.

GV1196.A52A3 2005
796.812'092—dc22
[B]
                                                            2005041845

This book is available in quantity at special discounts for your group or organization. For further information, contact:

Triumph Books
542 South Dearborn Street
Suite 750
Chicago, Illinois 60605
(312) 939-3330
Fax (312) 663-3557

Printed in U.S.A.

ISBN-13: 978-1-57243-730-2
ISBN-10: 1-57243-730-8

Design by Sue Knopf
Cover design by Concialdi Design

A Note from Adnan

Adnan will be donating a portion of his royalties to the newly created Adnan's Iraqi Children's Charity Foundation (AICCF). Please send donations to:

AICCF
P.O. Box 783
Hopkins, MN 55343

Thank you for your support.

Contents

Preface

Cavéat Emptor

(That's Latin for Buyer Beware . . .)

THE VIEWS AND OPINIONS EXPRESSED IN THIS BOOK are solely my own, Adnan Alkaissy's, and not those of the book's editor, Ross Bernstein, nor its publisher, Triumph Books. My goal in writing this book is to tell the world of my incredible journey from Iraq to America. Along the way I hope to both educate and entertain you with stories that range from being heartwarming to hilarious to downright unbelievable. Ultimately, my wish is to bring Americans and Muslims closer together in their work toward peace in this post–9-11 world. Please forgive me and accept my modest apology if you find any factual or historical inaccuracies inside. I am not a historian, but I do my best to tell the stories of Iraq and professional wrestling as I personally experienced them. I do not speak the best English, so bear with me while I try to tell you my amazing but true story. Hopefully, you will have half as much fun reading about it as I have had living it.

Acknowledgments

In addition to thanking my family and friends, I also want to thank all of my colleagues in the world of professional wrestling who have helped me in my career over the years. I have always tried to do my best and have really enjoyed being able to give back to my community. It is very important to me. So many people have been there for me over the years, and this is truly the least I can do in return. I couldn't do it without a lot of help, though, and there are two people in particular who I would like to acknowledge, Jeff Kuelbs and Mike Simmons. They are great guys who have really been instrumental in helping further my career in Minnesota. They have worked very hard to line up sponsors for me and also to help my charity shows become very successful. I am so grateful to people like that who have really gone out of their way to make my life more meaningful, and I just hope that I can do the same for others.

Introduction

UNBELIEVABLE. That was, in a word, my initial reaction to the story of Adnan Alkaissy. I first met Adnan while in the midst of writing a coffee-table book about the history of Minnesota wrestling and rassling last summer. My telephone rang one day, and innocently enough the voice on the other end said in a deep Arabic accent, "Hello, Ross, this is the sheikh." My mental Rolodex kicked into high gear at that point, but I could not figure out for the life of me who it was. Figuring it was one of my old fraternity buddies pulling a prank on me, I played along. But when he said it was "Sheikh Adnan Alkaissy, you know, the professional wrestler." I put two and two together.

Adnan had heard about my book project and wanted to get together to tell me his story. Normally I do most of my interviewing over the phone, but how often do you get to meet a sheikh? It was a total guilty pleasure—I mean, I grew up watching this guy on TV—so I agreed.

We met at a nearby restaurant, where he proceeded to tell me a little bit about himself. Ten minutes into our conversation, I was hanging on his every word. In fact, I could hardly believe my ears. Could it be true? Could it be possible that the guy sitting across from me, the lovable villain of Saturday night *All-Star Wrestling*, had actually grappled in front of hundreds of thousands of screaming fans back in his native Baghdad for none other than the infamous Saddam Hussein? The stories of murder and mayhem back in Iraq under Saddam were intoxicating, as was the saga of his ensuing escape to America. But why hadn't I heard about this incredible story before?

Adnan then told me that because Saddam was at long last in U.S. custody, and he no longer felt that he or his family back in Iraq were in danger, he could finally tell his story. And what a story it was. Originally expecting to write a brief chapter about his wrestling career in Minnesota for my book, I was floored when he asked me to write his biography.

I've authored more than 30 books, and this wasn't the first time I have been asked to write someone else's story. While I usually respectfully decline those offers, however, this one touched me in a different way. So I called my publisher in Chicago and pitched them the idea. They were sold.

With that, I spent the next six months getting to know the real Adnan Alkaissy. In fact, the sheikh is nothing like his bad-guy television persona. The real Adnan who I have gotten to know is a family man, a philanthropic man, and a man concerned about the future of his homeland back in Iraq. Now in his sixties, he is still quite a character and even gets into the ring on the weekends to entertain his legions of loyal fans.

The finished product is something we are both very proud of, and hopefully it will make a difference in this post–9-11 world. The current state of affairs in the Middle East is tumultuous at best right now, and hopefully the voice of an Iraqi American known by millions might just provide a small ray of hope in the quest for peace.

While the book is a very odd juxtaposition of two very different worlds, so is Adnan's life story. On one hand there are hilarious tales of what life was like both in and out of the circle of professional wrestling. On the other are stories of heartache and despair about a man whose country is once again trying to find itself. Mixed in are truly amazing stories that will make you laugh as well as make you cry.

This is a true story about a man's journey across two continents that has finally come full circle. It is also about a man's desire to obtain a sense of closure while telling his personal accounts about a separate life lived many years ago. Finally, it is a story about a man who wants nothing more than to go home to a free and democratic Iraq, where he can introduce his new family to his old one.

In many ways this is an unbelievable rags-to-riches-to-rags story about wrestling as a metaphor for life. I learned a great deal about the world I live in while writing this book, and in the end I hope that it will serve as a small catalyst of sorts to perhaps open a dialogue for all of us to better understand one another and just get along. That is what it is all about.

—*Ross Bernstein*

1

A Boy in Baghdad

WELCOME. MY NAME IS ADNAN Bin Abdulkareem
Ahmed Alkaissy El Farthie, and I was born on March 1, 1939.
In the heart of ancient Mesopotamia, the cradle of humanity,
lies my homeland—Iraq, the birthplace of humanity. I was raised
the youngest of five children in a district of Baghdad known
as Almahdia, a prominent region that is comprised of people
of the Sunni faith.

The two oldest children in my family were Fuad and Jalil,
both of whom were half brothers born to the first of my father's
two wives. (Taking more than one wife is a common practice
in Islamic culture.) However, when their mother was unable
to have any more children, my father met and married my birth
mother, Tarffa Salh. My mother and father then had three
more children: Kamil, who became a well-known judge

appointed by Saddam Hussein; Bahija, my sister; and me. Fuad and Jalil's mother, meanwhile, continued to live with us and was like a second mother to me (a practice that is common in my culture). We had a large extended family as well. Between my father's three brothers and my mother's six siblings, there were always plenty of aunts, uncles, and cousins around to play with.

We were raised in a very strict but loving manner, and growing up we did not have a lot of money. My father's salary as a religious leader was probably around 50 dinars a month, or about $120 U.S. Sometimes it was tough. We didn't have an ice box, a refrigerator, or even a stove. Sometimes we had no electricity and had to use kerosene lamps, but we managed. We were happy, and were grateful for what we did have. My parents did what they thought was best for our family, and they provided for us as well as they could.

My father, Alhaj Abdulkareem Ahmed Alkaissy, was the *imam*, or spiritual leader, of the Almahdia Mosque in Baghdad.

A prominent sheikh, he taught grammar and religious studies at several schools as well. (There are two kinds of sheikhs: the stereotypical Hollywood prince type, who typically inherit great wealth from royalty, and the religious

My father, a prominent Sunni Muslim cleric.

type, who are the equivalent of a high-ranking priest or bishop in Christianity. My father was the second type, and as the son of a sheikh, I, too, am allowed to use this title.) In addition to teaching, my father issued Fatwas, or religious laws, several times during the year and was one of the most respected religious figures in all of Baghdad. He was a very dedicated and courageous man who worked hard tending to the needs of others, and he had a huge impact on my life.

Another person who had a great influence on my life was my father's brother, Kassim Alkaissy. Uncle Kassim was one of the greatest religious leaders in all of Iraq. He was a renowned author and teacher at the al-Gaylani Mosque and was highly respected throughout the country. Whenever there was a problem with the rival tribal leaders, he was usually called in to make

> We were raised in a very strict but loving manner, and growing up we did not have a lot of money . . . but we managed. We were happy, and were grateful for what we did have.

the peace. He was a very important person, no question about it. And because he was my uncle, I was respected among my peers, and that went a long way with me being successful in school and in athletics. I will never forget when he died in the mid-fifties; his funeral was one of the largest in Iraqi history. There were thousands and thousands of people who came out to pay their respects to him. The mass of people actually carried his coffin on their shoulders for more than 15 miles through the city to his burial spot. It was incredible and made quite an impression on me. Growing up, I tried hard to follow his and my father's examples.

As a young boy I was very interested in sports. Whatever it was, I wanted to do it. I loved wrestling, soccer, swimming, volleyball, and weightlifting. My father used to tell me to quit playing sports because it wasn't going to earn me any money. He wanted me to get into religion, as he had, to earn an honest living. But I didn't want to do that; that just wasn't me. He also encouraged me to study hard and go to college, and that was something I would later be very grateful for.

I learned a lot of discipline from my father. I will never forget one time when I was 12 years old and playing soccer near the Royal Kingdom Cemetery in Baghdad with some of my friends. We got hungry, so I climbed a tree to get some dates. Well, this guy who worked there came over and yelled at me for climbing the tree and taking the dates. I apologized, but he got right in my face. I didn't want to look cowardly in front of my friends, so I punched him and really beat the hell out of him. I broke his nose, and he was bleeding everywhere. The next day at school the principal called me out in front of the entire student body, which had gathered for an assembly. He had a bamboo stick

> My father used to tell me to quit playing sports because it wasn't going to earn me any money. He wanted me to get into religion, as he had, to earn an honest living. But I didn't want to do that; that just wasn't me.

4

in his hand and looked very upset. He then held up the man's bloody T-shirt and asked me if I was the one who had done this. I was busted, so I confessed. I took responsibility for it and said that we were just hungry, but that the guy had challenged me so I felt that I had to defend my honor. Honor is very important in the Arabic culture, and I felt like I was being insulted. Meanwhile, they had called my father to come down, and he entered the room. By then I was terrified. I told my dad that I was sorry, but he didn't say a word. He just looked at me disappointedly. So, they sat me down and took my shoes off. Two teachers held me down while my father whipped the bottom of my feet with that bamboo stick. I cried and cried—it was the worst pain I had ever experienced. I begged him to stop and promised that I would never do anything like that again. I was bleeding when my father finally stopped, and I couldn't even walk. The teachers then gave a big speech to all the students, using me as an example.

As I was hobbling home, a kid from school came up to me and started teasing me about what had happened. I told him to leave me alone, but he didn't. So I smacked him right in the nose and dropped him. He ran off crying. I knew that I might have gotten in trouble again at that point, but I knew that I had to defend my honor—to me it was something worth taking a beating for. I realized that taking the dates in a sacred cemetery was wrong, but punching some idiot who wanted to rub it in my face was fine by me.

I loved my father and respected him for what he had to do. It was a tough, humiliating lesson, but one that I never forgot.

After graduating from elementary school, I went on to attend junior high school in Baghdad. I was 6' by the time I was 13 years old and had developed into a pretty good athlete. I had a lot of friends and was very well known in my school. I also enjoyed the competition of playing sports and had success early on, which gave me a lot of self-confidence. I played soccer because I had very strong legs, and I loved to lift weights, but wrestling was my favorite sport by far. Wrestling was huge in the Middle East. At the high school and Olympic levels it was right up there with soccer in terms of popularity.

As a wrestler I won a lot of tournaments throughout the area and was one of the top competitors in my weight division. We even competed in neighboring countries, including Iran, where I met the infamous shah of Iran, Mohammad Reza Pahlavi, at a meet. I will never forget that meet. The arena was packed to the rafters and we were all very intimidated. Iran had the best wrestlers in the world at the time because the shah loved the sport and used to reward his top competitors with all kinds of riches. If they won a gold medal in the Olympics, he would give them a new house, a new car, and even a new job working for the government with a big salary. If a wrestler won gold, he was set for life, so they had a lot of incentive to succeed over there.

So we were at this tournament against the Iranians and every single person on my team had lost leading up to my final match as the heavyweight. I can still remember my opponent's name, Muhamadie—he was huge. It was incredible. The crowd was screaming at him not to run around so much and to face me. They were screaming, "Shame on you for running from Alkaissy. . . ." I wound up beating him by one point on a dramatic reversal in the final seconds. Afterward I met the shah, and he gave me a medal for winning the meet. I can only imagine what happened to Muhamadie after that; he probably got punished for losing to me.

I continued to enjoy my schooling and participating in athletics after that. Being a boy in Baghdad at that time was fun. Life was an adventure, and I never knew what was going to happen next. When school started back up the next fall, I met a young man who would forever change my life.

The crowd was screaming, . . . "Shame on you for running from Alkaissy. . . ." I wound up beating him by one point on a dramatic reversal in the final seconds.

2

Meeting a Young Man Named Saddam

I FIRST MET SADDAM HUSSEIN when I was in junior high school. He was a year older than I was, but we had many activities together and became friends. Saddam was a tall, lanky kid and pretty much kept to himself. He was very polite, very nice, wore nice clothes, and was really sort of shy. He was also very smart. He always had a book or newspaper with him wherever he went; he always wanted to be reading and learning. And he was very interested in Middle Eastern politics and current events; that is what he liked to talk about.

We didn't really play any sports together. He liked volleyball and basketball, and I was into soccer and wrestling. But we used to hang out after school together at a little open-air coffee shop near the Tigris River in Baghdad. There, we played dominos, chess, cards, and would sit around and watch TV or listen to music with our friends. It was a lot of fun.

At the time, the Baath Party was just coming to power in Iraq, and they were recruiting people pretty aggressively, especially students. Joining the party was a very popular thing to do back then, and most of the people that I knew were joining up. Saddam, meanwhile, was the perfect candidate. He came from a broken home and was in search of something more for himself. It is amazing to think about, but you could tell even early on that he had a plan. He was determined to get involved somehow, and this was the first step on his long journey to power and tyranny.

> At the time, the Baath Party was just coming to power in Iraq, and they were recruiting people pretty aggressively, especially students. . . . Saddam, meanwhile, was the perfect candidate. . . . It is amazing to think about, but you could tell even early on that he had a plan.

Although we may never really understand Saddam, understanding where he came from helps. Saddam was a Sunni Muslim who grew up in the northern city of Tikrit, Iraq. His father died when he was a boy and I think that had a profound effect on him. He had a tough childhood; there's no question about that. He didn't have any brothers or sisters that he was close to, so after his father's death he was raised by his uncle, Khairallah Talfah, who lived in Baghdad. His uncle was well-to-do and had money, however, so Saddam had nice things. Saddam's mother later remarried, but I don't think that he ever really came to terms with it. He became a loner and expressed his anger and frustration through his pursuit of knowledge. He wanted to learn as much as possible because he knew that knowledge was the basis of power.

Saddam and I both grew up in the Adhamia district of Baghdad. I wound up attending Adhamia High School; however, Saddam eventually transfered to nearby Alkarah High School. He got into a lot of trouble at Adhamia, and I think that is why he switched schools. He had become more and more involved in politics and by then was very loyal to the Baath Party. I will never forget one story about Saddam that I heard when I was a little older. Apparently, there was a Communist Party member who became the mayor of Tikrit, Saddam's hometown. Saddam hated the Communists, so this did not sit well with him at all. He went back to Tikrit one day and he shot the guy. He was probably only 16 years old at the time, but he was fearless. He was a loyal Baathist and hated the Communists with a passion. The Communists were the rival political arm to the Baathists and were very powerful at the time. Saddam was a religious person, however, and felt it was the right thing to do for both himself and his party. Everyone I knew was shocked that he would do that. He didn't care about going to jail or anything; he just wanted to make a statement. He served only six months in jail for it though, because his uncle had a lot of pull and got him out.

Saddam was one tough SOB, and nobody messed with him. After the shooting, people knew that he meant business, and he gained a lot of respect. Most people were scared to death of him. I think that the writing was on the wall at this point in regard to Saddam getting into politics—he had shown that he would do just about anything for a cause in which he believed. That type of selfless attitude was just the sort of thing that the Baathists were searching for at the time, and that is why he quickly rose up through their ranks.

> Saddam was one tough SOB, and nobody messed with him. . . . He had shown that he would do just about anything for a cause in which he believed.

After Saddam transferred to a different school I didn't see him very often. But I still ran into him at the local coffee shop, and we were always friendly toward one another. We played dominos and talked about politics and religion for the most part. I remember finally asking him about his time in jail and about why he shot that guy, but he didn't want to talk about it too much. He was a very private person.

I could see that there was a lot of hatred brewing in Iraq at the time, and it was getting pretty scary. In fact, as a young man I witnessed first hand two separate revolutions that really had an impact on my life. The first revolution happened during an attempted coup. I had just started high school, and I remember leaving school with a bunch of my friends and walking home together. All hell broke loose when we tried to cross a bridge over the Tigris River in Baghdad. We had to get over the bridge to get home, and when we were halfway across it we saw three military figures on top of a balcony at a mosque with machine guns. So we just started running as fast as we could. I lost my shoes because I was running so fast. Then, so help me God, I looked over and saw three of my classmates get shot right next to me as we were running. I can honestly say I have never been more afraid of anything in my entire life. I thought I was going to die, and I can remember thinking about what it would feel like to get shot. I just kept running, and when I got home I realized that my clothes were covered in blood. That's how close I was to my friends when they got shot. I told my mom what happened and she just cried. It was unbelievable. I was so sad for my friends who died; I felt hopeless. The funerals were the next day, because in Islamic law the bodies must be buried within 24 hours. We were all just devastated. I couldn't understand what was happening to my country.

The second revolution I experienced came a few years later when King Faisal and his family were captured and killed. I was very sad because I could remember being with my parents as a child and seeing him ride through the streets of Baghdad on his horse and carriage in elaborate ceremonies. He was a well-respected man at the time. And sadly, more than just he and his family were lost. Other members of his cabinet were also captured and tortured during this era and were even hung upside down in the streets of Baghdad. Blood was all over the place, and it was a very scary time.

By then I had finished high school and wanted to get away. I just knew that I needed to get out of there before I wound up like my friends on the bridge. I can remember seeing Saddam right after that and talking to him in a coffee shop. There I was, terrified that the country was going to hell, and there he was, very calm and quiet. It was as if he knew what was going on and was enjoying it. He and I had very different outlooks on life. I wanted to go to college and see the world. I was interested in sports, girls, and having fun. Saddam, meanwhile, was all business, and was more interested in getting into politics and government affairs. I remember him scoffing at me when I told him what I wanted to do. He had much bigger plans in life and was eager to begin his rise to the top. As I said, we had very different outlooks on life. And I was ready to get out of the unstable, dangerous Iraq and try my hand at the American dream.

> I was ready to get out of the unstable, dangerous Iraq and try my hand at the American dream.

3

Coming to America

AFTER HIGH SCHOOL I WAS ANXIOUS TO TRAVEL and see the world. Luckily, there was an organization called the American Friends of the Middle East that had a big office in Baghdad. I had heard about them from some friends of mine, so I went to check them out. The recruiter I met with there took a real liking to me and came to a lot of my athletic events. This group was determined to get the top kids in Baghdad to continue their educations over in America. They recruited the best kids to get athletic scholarships and probably figured that down the road those kids would be great resources for both intelligence and diplomacy. I don't know if that was the case for sure, but I really didn't care; I was just thrilled that I was going to get a college education and that I was going to America.

In any case, that guy really helped me out with the paper-work and took me under his wing. He even invited me over to his house, which was like a palace, and he really made the trip to America happen for me. I appreciated his help because my time in America changed my life. He told me that I had a bright future and that America was the place for someone like me to be. I really wanted to go overseas to study and see what it was all about, so I jumped at the opportunity. Incredibly, with his help, I got a football scholarship to the University of Houston. What was so amazing about getting a football scholarship was the fact that the only football I had ever played at the time was what Americans call soccer. I was a very good soccer player in high school, but I had no idea how to play American football—none whatsoever. I suppose they figured that because I was a good soccer player I could be their field-goal kicker. Ironically, I wound up playing line-backer instead. To tell you the truth, I didn't care where I played; I was just excited to be getting out of Iraq and the polit-ical mess there. I was going to America, and I just couldn't wait for the adventure to begin. I couldn't wait to get there and see everything that I had heard about and read about in books. It was a dream come true for me. I didn't have a dime in my pocket at the time, but I didn't care. The University of

> What was so amazing about getting a football scholarship was the fact that the only football I had ever played at the time was what Americans call soccer.

Houston told me that they would get me a job, and that was good enough for me. Because my family was poor and didn't have a lot of money, it was a real break for us.

Once we got all the logistics worked out, I packed up and said good-bye. It was going to be the trip of a lifetime. From Baghdad I took a bus through Syria to Lebanon and then boarded a ship to Italy. From there, we transferred to a train through France and got on another ship to cross the English Channel. Unfortunately, I got a nasty infection in my leg and had to spend 10 days in a hospital in London. I didn't speak very good English, so that was tough. When I got better I boarded a ship across the Atlantic to New York. It was amazing; the ship was so big and there were so many interesting people on board. That is where I caught my first break.

One afternoon I was exercising in the workout room and this big guy who was about 6'4" and 280 pounds walked in with a couple of hot blondes. I looked at him and thought, "Oh my God, who in the hell is this guy? He's just ripped!" It turned out to be Yvonne Robert, a famous professional wrestler who was the reigning World Heavyweight Champion at the time.

He looked at me, saw my cauliflower ears, and said, "You're a wrestler. Where are you from?" "Baghdad," I said. And then I told him I was on my way to Houston to play college football. So he told me that he knew the main professional wrestling promoter in Houston very well and that he would put in a good word for me if I wanted to get into that sort of thing down the road. I didn't know the first thing about pro wrestling at the time, but figured anybody who looked like that was someone

I wanted to hang around with—and the girls too! I figured sure, why not.

Then he asked me if I wanted him to show me some wrestling moves. I agreed, thinking it would be fun. We found some mats and squared up right there in the exercise room. Wanting to impress his girlfriends, he lunged right at me. I then countered him, dove for his legs, picked him up, and threw him on his back. His eyes were about the size of basketballs at that point. I didn't realize it then, but he didn't know a thing about amateur wrestling. He started screaming, "Take it easy, kid!" I didn't know any better, so he told me to be gentle, but make it look painful. It was my very first lesson in professional wrestling and something I never forgot. We hung out together on the ship after that, and he kind of took me under his wing. It was wonderful. He always had a gorgeous blonde on his arm wherever he went, and I was along for the ride. I was just in awe of the guy. I wasn't even in America yet and already I was living like a rock star. I couldn't wait to get there.

> Wanting to impress his girlfriends, he lunged right at me. I then countered him, dove for his legs, picked him up, and threw him on his back. . . . He started screaming, "Take it easy, kid!"

When we got to New York, Yvonne took me in his car to show me around town. He even introduced me to legendary boxer Jack Dempsey at his restaurant down on Broadway. I couldn't believe it. I ate my first steak there and thought that

that was what America was all about. I was here to stay. Two days later Yvonne put me on a bus to Texas, and we shook hands and said good-bye. He gave me his number, though, and told me to stay in touch. (I did, and we later became good friends when I got into the business.) I left hoping all Americans were as nice as my new friend, Yvonne.

4

The All-American Boy

THE BUS RIDE FROM NEW YORK TO TEXAS was long but very interesting. I saw a lot of things I had never seen before and couldn't believe how much wide open space there was. The bus stopped in all of these small towns, and oftentimes we would get off the bus to stretch our legs. Just seeing the different cars, the clothes people were wearing, the farms, the animals, and the different kinds of architecture from place to place was fascinating. It was an education just taking that bus across the country. There were so many different cultures and races. It was all new and exciting. When I finally got to Houston I was really excited. I couldn't wait to meet my new roommate and get acclimated to the campus. I was nervous about being able to speak English well enough, but just figured that I would learn it on the fly.

One of the first things that I did when I arrived was meet the football coaches. They were impressed with my physique but not so much with my understanding of the game. After I realized how much more difficult it was to kick a football than it was to kick a soccer ball, I felt more at home playing linebacker. It was pretty basic—just tackle the guy with the ball. With my wrestling background I did very well at that position and found myself really enjoying the game. My teammates were very nice and helped me better understand the rules, too, which I greatly appreciated.

As far as school went, it was tough but fun. My freshman year was memorable, and I really had a good time learning about American culture. I loved living in the dormitory and meeting all the girls. I could see why so many people wanted to come to America—there were so many opportunities for those who were willing to work hard and pay the price for success.

The next summer almost the entire football coaching staff left to coach at Southern Methodist University in Dallas. It was a big ordeal and it meant big changes for the entire program. I was really sad because I had grown very close to several members of the staff. That next fall when the team hit the field it was a totally different atmosphere. I didn't particularly like the new coaches and could tell right away that I was probably not going to fit into their playbook. So I took a huge leap of faith and decided to transfer to Oklahoma State University and walk on to the wrestling team. Houston didn't have a wrestling program, and that was really my passion, not football. I had written to the OSU coaches and told them my story about being a successful amateur wrestler back in Iraq. They wrote me back and said they would give me a shot if I was willing to transfer. It was a big risk, though, to leave my scholarship behind. I didn't have any money, but I figured I could earn a scholarship there if I made the squad. That was the beauty of wrestling: if you could beat the guy ahead of you on the depth chart, you took his spot. It is a very fair sport in that regard. Football, on the other hand, came down to politics and whether or not the coach wanted to start you or bench you. I couldn't take that kind of pressure in Houston and didn't want to sit on the bench all year waiting to get cut, so I packed up and left.

Stillwater, Oklahoma, was a very nice place, and I could tell that I was going to enjoy living in a smaller town. When I got there I began training to make the wrestling team right away. I

> That was the beauty of wrestling: if you could beat the guy ahead of you on the depth chart, you took his spot.

was desperate and knew that my future depended on getting that scholarship. When I got to the first practice I saw that the current heavyweight was pretty good. He was also 300 pounds: much bigger than I was. The coaches threw us on the mat together and let us go at it. Luckily, I was much quicker than he was, and I wound up beating him right away to earn my spot on the roster. In fact, the guy was so upset over losing his spot that he quit. Presto, I had my scholarship.

It was great to be wrestling competitively again, and I was having a lot of fun. OSU was a great school, and I really had a good time there. I met a lot of nice people and even joined a fraternity. So many girls, so many parties—this was what college life was all about. I felt a million miles away from home and couldn't even imagine going back at that point. My English was improving and my grades were decent, too. It was a great opportunity for me, and I was truly very happy.

I had learned all about pro wrestling while I was in college and figured I could make a living doing it. If nothing else, I thought I could at least make a few bucks and maybe meet a few gorgeous blondes as Yvonne had.

Eventually, I wound up wrestling down a weight class at 191 pounds. It was nice to drop some weight and not have to try to battle those 300-pound giants. My teammates were great guys, and I fit right in. We were very good together, too. In fact, for two years we were the best in the country. That's right, our Cowboy squad won the NCAA National Championship in 1958 and 1959, my sophomore and junior seasons. I was on top of the world. It was great to see all of my hard work and dedication pay off. I ended up winning a national AAU individual title, finished third at the 1959 NCAA National Tournament, and even earned All-American honors.

During my senior year I started to think about what I wanted to do with my life. I was working toward my degree in education and figured that a career as a teacher and coach would suit me well. Things were going well both on and off the mat, but my biggest problem was the fact that I didn't have any money. It

This is me as a young grappler just starting out in Portland, Oregon.

was tough to not be able to do many of the things my teammates and friends were doing. Most of the kids were there because their parents were paying the bills. I was not so fortunate, and to be honest I was tired of not being able to go on nice dates or drive my own car.

I decided to call my old friend Yvonne Robert. He then put me in touch with his friend, the professional wrestling promoter back in Houston. I called him, told him who I was, and he invited me down for a tryout. I was all set. I had learned all about pro wrestling while I was in college and figured I could make a living doing it. If nothing else, I thought I could at least make a few bucks and maybe meet a few gorgeous blondes as Yvonne had. So I took another leap of faith and left Oklahoma State in the middle of my senior year. I was a few semesters short of graduating but figured I could do that later. I was on my way to becoming a big star . . . or so I thought.

5

Enter "the Chief"

WHEN I GOT TO HOUSTON I met up with promoters Morris Sigal and Paul Bauch. They were impressed with my size and my looks—both of which are very important in pro wrestling. They knew that I was a good amateur wrestler but didn't know if I had the dynamic personality necessary to become a successful entertainer. Pro wrestling was completely different than amateur wrestling, and I definitely had my work cut out for me.

Pro wrestling, like everything else in Texas, was big. They took it very seriously down there, and in the early sixties it was universally understood that it was all real. You see, even though many speculated that wrestling was fake, there was a strict code of silence amongst the performers that protected the industry's most sacred trade secrets and kept up the illusion of reality.

THE SHEIKH OF BAGHDAD

Aside from the wrestlers, refs, and promoters, only a chosen few were part of the backstage fraternity known as the inner circle. It was a code based largely on the traditions dating back to the old carnival days of the late 1800s, by which no one dared question their validity . . . or else. Should anyone dare say the F-word (fake), there would be hell to pay. Someone who broke the code would be blackballed, never allowed to work in wrestling again, or perhaps even worse things. So I not only had to learn how to perform in the ring, but I also had to learn how to perform well enough to convince all the fans that it was 100 percent legit.

> There was a strict code of silence amongst the performers that protected the industry's most sacred trade secrets and kept up the illusion of reality. . . . Should anyone dare say the F-word (fake), there would be hell to pay.

When I first started out my gimmick wasn't much of a stretch for me—I just wrestled under my own name and wore my University of Houston Cougars football uniform. I was portrayed as a good guy, or "babyface." The villains were the other guys, known as "heels," and that was what wrestling was all about: good versus evil. The fans loved it. The promoters basically decided how each match was going to go down and from there it was up to us to make it as entertaining as possible. The better the storylines that we came up with, the better the attendance. The more people that showed up, the more money we made. I figured out pretty quickly that I needed to work well with my opponent in the ring in order to make it look really good.

Once I got a few matches under my belt, it was easy. I didn't realize it at the time, but I was a natural. I loved to entertain the crowd, and I loved the feeling I got when the referee raised my hand in victory. Sure, it wasn't real, but the crowd didn't know that. It was entertainment, and I was an entertainer. It was really exciting to see how you could manipulate the crowd to do just about anything. You could get them all to either cheer for you or boo the other guy; it was something else. I mean to have so many people right at your fingertips was very exciting.

As a wrestler I did some tag-team matches with an old football buddy of mine from Houston, Hogan Wharton. In that act we wore our old Houston Cougars jerseys and tackled our opponents in the ring. They loved football down in Texas, and it went over big. We made a lot of money together traveling around Texas and had a really good time, too. Meanwhile, when I wanted to get away and relax I went to my old college roommate's house, Jim Harding, who lived in Amarillo, Texas. His entire family took me in and really made me feel like I had a home. They were wonderful people.

I stayed in Houston for a little over a year and then moved to Portland, Oregon, to join a different promotion. I was ready to try something different and it seemed like a good opportunity. Back then guys used to move around to different "territories" a lot. The promoters loved to get fresh meat in their territories in order to give their fans some new characters either to cheer for or boo.

When I got there I decided that I might as well finish my degree at nearby Portland State University. I enrolled as a student and also served as an assistant coach for the school's wrestling team. I met with the promoter Don Owen, who told me that he needed an Indian for his promotion. He had arranged for another guy to come in as an Indian, but that guy never showed up, so he asked me if I wanted to do it. I said, "Sure." So they came up with the name "Chief Billy White Wolf" for me, and it stuck. Because I was a pro, however, I couldn't wrestle as an amateur anymore. But just being around the college team was nice because it kept me in great shape. It was fun being back on a campus and going to classes again. I would wrestle a few nights a week and make some money and then study the rest of the time; it was a nice setup.

I got my degree about a year later and after that transferred to the University of Oregon, in Eugene, where I got my master's degree in education. The school's administration even encouraged me to go for my doctorate so that I would be in a position to take over as the head wrestling coach when the then-current coach retired in a couple of years. I started to take classes toward my degree and meanwhile I was still wrestling professionally as Chief Billy White Wolf. I was well on my way toward capturing my fourth National Wrestling Alliance (NWA) Pacific Northwest Tag Team Title. Things were going very well for me at that point.

I traveled to other territories as well, including those down South and on the East Coast. Traveling was a huge part of wrestling and it got to be a grind. But if you were a single guy and didn't mind all the road trips, it could be fun and interesting. I met a lot of colorful characters, that was for sure. In

Here I am as half of the WWWF championship tag team alongside Chief Jay Strongbow (on left).

fact, one of the most interesting people I ever worked with was a guy by the name of Haystacks Calhoun. We worked as tag-team partners in Connecticut for a few weeks back in the early sixties. Haystacks was a huge, 600-pound, Southern redneck hillbilly who always wore big bib overalls—in and out of the ring—because that is probably all that fit him. I went over to his house one time to pick him up for a match, and I saw him outside playing with this tiny little wiener dog puppy. He told me that he and his wife fell in love with the puppy and had bought him that morning at the pet store.

When I went back to pick him up for a match again the next day, he was sitting outside in the same spot crying like a baby. "What's wrong, big man? You look like somebody died,"

I said. He told me that when they got up that morning they couldn't find their little dog anywhere and were worried that he might have somehow gotten loose. But after his wife, who was about 300 pounds herself, started to make the bed, she discovered the dog lying on the mattress—flat as a pancake. I tried not to laugh, but I couldn't help myself. Apparently the dog got in bed with them and Haystacks rolled over on the little fella. He was beside himself, but I encouraged him to get a big dog next time, and that is exactly what he did. I told him to have the dog sleep in a dog house, too, and he looked at me, laughing, and said, "I think you're right!"

> After his wife, who was about 300 pounds herself, started to make the bed, she discovered the dog lying on the mattress—flat as a pancake.

I eventually came to the conclusion that trying to get my doctorate and advance my career as a wrestler at the same time was becoming too difficult. Plus, I was running out of money to pay for everything. I had to make a career choice. I had gotten a good offer to go over to Japan and wrestle there for a while, so I took it. I was anxious to try something new and knew I wouldn't miss studying all the time.

Incidentally, another hilarious situation involving my old friend Haystacks took place on a flight to Tokyo. In fact, it might be the funniest memory that I have from all my years of pro wrestling. Back then when you flew to the Far East you had to fly from Minneapolis to L.A., over to Hawaii, on to

Fiji, and then to Japan. You had to refuel at every stop, and it took an entire day to get there. It was very boring to say the least, so we drank a lot of cocktails and talked BS with the guys to make the time go by faster.

On this particular flight there was a big group of wrestlers from the United States making the trip. Pro wrestling was huge in Japan and they loved us over there. Haystacks was going to be billed by the promoters as the "up and coming American sumo giant" and was really excited about getting there and talking to the media. This was his first overseas flight, though, and he got some great news when he boarded the plane: because he couldn't fit into the seats back in coach, he was getting bumped up to first class. So while the rest of us wrestlers sat back in coach, Haystacks was up in front being wined and dined. Remember, at the time first class was very opulent and you could eat and drink as much as you wanted. Well, every time the big fella got a glass of champagne, he would look back and tease us mercilessly. Haystacks, whose diet at the time consisted primarily of basic down-home country food, was gorging himself on caviar, salmon, and fine wine—all things that his enormous stomach had never seen the likes of before. He just kept eating and drinking, taunting us along the way until he could eat no more. At that point, we could hear him moaning up there, and it was loud. All of that rich food was about to make its way back toward the exits.

At that point, Haystacks got up to use the bathroom, only to find he couldn't fit in there. He tried and tried, but he could not get his big butt in. By then the stewardesses were trying to help him, but they realized that they were going to have to escort him all the way to the back of the plane where the galley was. As he was walking back through the plane, he started getting stomach cramps and let out a huge fart. It was awful. Meanwhile, we were all just dying of laughter and couldn't control ourselves.

He got back there, and the stewardesses emptied out an old burlap mail sack for him. They then tied it up on both sides, held up a blanket to give him some privacy, and let him take care of his business. At that point it was coming out of both ends and was loud—very loud. A lot of the passengers were horrified at what they were seeing, hearing, and smelling. It was horrible.

Finally, after about 20 minutes, the stewardesses escorted him back to his seat. He had to walk right past all of us and was so embarrassed. He literally had to shift his stomach from one side to the other in between each seat to get down the aisle. I felt terrible for him. But he was ribbing and teasing us the whole way, so we knew that he was all right. As he walked past us, we saw that his bib overall straps were hanging behind him and his ass was wet from where he crapped his pants. We just about lost it at that point. On top of all that, two petite Japanese stewardesses were walking in front of and behind him spraying perfume atomizers all over as he walked by. That poor bastard was really a mess.

We got to Tokyo and the Japanese media was everywhere and wanted to take pictures of Haystacks. As we got off the plane a reporter came running up to him and asked him how his first flight to Japan was. Old Haystacks went off on that guy like I had never before seen anyone go off. You see, he thought that we had put the reporter up to it, so he cussed him out

Applying my signature move, the Indian Death Lock, while wrestling as Chief Billy White Wolf during a match in Hawaii.

like crazy, calling him every name in the book. When he realized that we hadn't, he wanted to crawl under a rock. He had to apologize to all of them—making his horrendous day even worse. That was one of the funniest incidents of my entire life, I will never forget it.

I wrestled as Chief Billy White Wolf in Japan, and the fans really liked me. I played a villain as well as a hero, and it was a lot of fun. In all I made about four or five trips overseas and found it to be a great change of pace. The culture was so different, and the people were nice. I think that because I was used to living in another part of the world I was able to adapt to Japan better than the American wrestlers did. For instance, I really enjoyed the food, whereas a lot of guys got sick from it. I also didn't mind sleeping on the floor. The American guys couldn't deal with the fact that toilets over there were nothing more than a hole in the ground. Well, that was what I grew up with back home. The promoters liked me because I never complained and just made the best of it. We toured the entire country, and the people were great to me wherever we went. In fact, being over there kind of made me homesick for Iraq.

6

Going Home
an Orphan

AFTER SPENDING SOME TIME IN JAPAN, I finally decided to go home and visit my family. It was 1963, I was 24 years old and, incredibly, I hadn't been back to Baghdad since I had left nearly seven years earlier. Sure, over the years I had written a lot of letters to my parents and siblings, but I could never afford to go back. To be able to go home with a master's degree and stories of a successful wrestling career was something I was very excited about. I couldn't wait to see my mom and dad; they were going to be so proud.

When I got home my brothers and their families all met me at the Baghdad airport. My older brothers were all very successful people, and I really looked up to them, so I was eager to see them and tell them about my achievements in America. It was an incredible homecoming for me—I was so excited to finally be home. I hugged everybody and then asked where my mom and dad were. My brother then told me that they were on vacation. I asked him when they were coming back, and he told me it would be a few days. I thought that was strange, but didn't think too much about it. Then, later that night back at my brother Kamil's house, they told me the whole story. My parents were dead. They had died in separate incidents less than a year apart more than three years prior.

I was absolutely devastated. I just cried and cried. I don't think I left my brother's house for a week. It was unbelievable that they had kept such a big secret from me for so many years. When I asked them why, they told me that they didn't want to upset me when I was in America doing so well. They figured that I would rush home and not finish my education. They were probably right. So, pretending to be my parents, they had actually answered the letters that I sent to my mom and dad. For all that time I didn't know my own parents were dead, and that was extremely difficult to accept. At first I was very mad at my brothers, but then I understood why they did it. They loved me, and they wanted what was best for me. They were trying to protect me. I eventually forgave them, but it took a while.

The story of my dad's death is difficult for me to think about. My dad was a deeply religious man and someone I greatly respected. There is a word in Islam called *Mutasarrif*, which means you have a very deep fundamental understanding of the Muslim religion and are considered to be extremely close to God. My father committed 100 percent of his life to God and to understanding and interpreting the Koran, as well as its *Sharia*, or laws, which were written by the Prophet Mohammed himself.

My father decided to go to Saudi Arabia on a Hajj. It is an amazing thing: every year nearly 5 million Muslims from around the world go to Mecca to have a spiritual awakening. It is believed that all Muslims must go to Mecca at least once in their lifetime in order to have their sins forgiven. My father strongly believed that once you did this you would live in the house of God forever. He ultimately decided to leave my family to spend his final days with God at Mecca. So he told my mother and brothers and sister that he wasn't coming home. They all cried, but he had made up his mind to leave and that was that.

> It is an amazing thing: every year nearly 5 million Muslims from around the world go to Mecca to have a spiritual awakening.

When my father arrived in Mecca, he spent a lot of his time learning about religion and enjoying himself. One day while he was marching to nearby Mount Arafat, he suffered a heat stroke and then passed away a short time later. He was buried right there in the holiest region of Saudi Arabia, Mecca. It was a very big honor. My family was sad, but happy that he was able to die on his own terms doing something he truly wanted to be doing. He was a great, great man. I miss him and think of him each and every day.

It was 1959 when my father died, and my mother passed away less than a year later. My sister told me that my mom used to cry night and day after I left for America. She was so upset that I moved away that she was never the same. I was very close to my mother, and I used to write her letters at least once a week. She apparently would wait at the post office for hours in anticipation of receiving my letters.

She eventually died of natural causes, but my siblings felt that my leaving home played a big part in her deteriorating health. My brother told me that in his opinion she died because she loved me so much—maybe too much. I was her baby boy, and she could never really let go. She would cry and cry when I was gone, and I guess that was very hard on her. Then, when my father died, that was probably just too much for her to handle. To think that my own mother died because of the pain I caused her by not being home for her is something very difficult to come to terms with. I still think about that and pray to her often. She was a truly wonderful lady.

7

The Winds of
Change Back Home

AFTER **I** GOT PAST THE INITIAL SHOCK of my
parents' deaths, I found it nice to be back with my siblings.
I met several new nieces and nephews and enjoyed getting
to know them. My siblings were highly respected in their
fields and had made good lives for themselves in Baghdad.
One brother was a lawyer, another worked as an accountant
at the Ministry of Communication, and the third was a judge.
My sister had a good husband and stayed home with her
children.

After being home for a while, I thought that it would be nice
to see some of my old high school friends. My brothers then
sat me down and told me that things had really changed in

the seven years since I had left. The Baath Party had come to power, and many of my old friends who had political affiliations with the opposition were literally in hiding. I couldn't believe it—the man behind much of the turmoil was my old friend, Saddam Hussein.

> The Baath Party had come to power, and many of my old friends who had political affiliations with the opposition were literally in hiding. I couldn't believe it— the man behind much of the turmoil was my old friend, Saddam Hussein.

At the time, President Abdul Karim Qassim had just been assassinated by the Baath Party, and it was a really trying time in Iraqi history. It was a terribly bloody coup planned by the Baathists along with a group of Arab Nationalists. More than two thousand Iraqis died during the uprising.

The Soviet Union was a strong ally of Iraq at the time, and the Iraqi Army had a lot of Russian MiGs. The MiGs were constantly flying over Baghdad; it was a really scary time. When it was all said and done, Qassim was handcuffed to a chair and then shot with machine guns on live television. It was incredible, almost too horrific to believe. His body started smoking from being shot at by so many thousands of bullets. I have never seen anything like that in my life; it was very upsetting. Saddam was not the main leader of the Baath Party at that point, but was clearly rising to power behind the scenes. He had emerged as one of the party's shining stars and was doing whatever he could to be in a position to one day take over.

Meanwhile, after being home for a few weeks, I was contacted by the local media. They wanted to do some stories about me, portraying me as a well-to-do young Iraqi who had achieved educational and professional success in America and come home again. I was featured on several national television and radio shows as well as on the front page of several newspapers. It was a thrill to be home and to have that kind of attention. They were also very intrigued with my career as a professional wrestler. Amateur wrestling was a big deal in Iraq, but pro wrestling was something new and different. As a result of all of the media attention, I was thrust into the limelight in a way I had never been before. All of a sudden everybody knew who I was and I was literally made into a sort of national hero. It was an honor.

I remember one time shortly after that when I was driving around with a friend, who was a member of the Baath Party, and a car pulled up alongside us. I could see that it was several members of the Communist Party. They were all wearing sunglasses and driving in a big black Mercedes. This type of hit squad was not uncommon in Iraq at the time. They were out to kill any Baath Party opposition that hadn't gone into hiding. I am pretty sure that he was on their short list of people to knock off. When they pulled up next to us at a stoplight, my friend looked at me, terrified, and said to just go and please get him out of there. But when I looked over at the car, they looked at me and nodded OK. They recognized me from being on TV and at that point I knew we were safe. It was unreal. My friend was so lucky that it worked out that way; otherwise he probably would have been killed.

Wanting to cash in on my newly found fame, I decided to stay in Iraq for a while longer. I was staying at my brother's house, and he assured me that I was welcome to stay as long as I wished. Believe it or not, I was even offered a high-level position in the Iraqi Army. I actually considered it for a while. I knew that with my education I could start out as an officer and then later work in the Ministry of Sports, which had always been a dream of mine. I had no intentions of signing a life term; rather, I figured I could stay for a year or two and see how it went. You could do that sort of thing back then. But after thinking about it and coming to my senses, I decided against it. It was just too difficult to be there and have to deal with everything that was going on politically at the time. To see the president die on live TV, that was too much, and I couldn't take it. Incredibly, the next president was assassinated just a few months later when his helicopter was blown up in Basra. Things were really bad back home, and they were getting worse.

What really put me over the edge and made me finally decide to return to America were all the pictures of my mom in my brother's house. It was just too tough to look at them. It was almost as if I could hear her talking to me from the dead. I had to get a hold of myself. I was having really bad nightmares, and I just wanted to get out of Iraq. To make matters worse, I was arguing with my brother's wife a lot. When I got to Iraq, I had wanted to do something nice for my siblings, so I bought them some nice things such as a new ice box and stove. I think my sister-in-law resented the fact that I was a little bit famous and had some money. Eventually I moved out and stayed at the Sahara Hotel in downtown Baghdad. Beyond all of that, it was summer at the time, and I couldn't stand the intense heat

My family back home.

because I had gotten used to the cool air in Oregon. There was no air conditioning anywhere, so it was tough. Ultimately, all of those things just piled up in my mind and after a couple of months I realized that I needed to get the hell out of Iraq.

I had gotten a good taste of Western culture and simply wanted to go back. I was making a nice living in pro wrestling and was not ready to settle down. I had started to make a name for myself back in America and figured that I could have a good future there. So I said good-bye once again and headed straight for the airport.

8

Feeling Like a Nomad

INCREDIBLY, WHEN I GOT TO THE AIRPORT my day turned bad. I was stopped by the police, arrested, handcuffed, and told that I was being charged with multiple counts of murder. Words couldn't even begin to describe how shocked I was at that very moment. I pleaded with them that they had the wrong person, but they would not listen to me. They then took me back to a holding cell to interrogate me. I was terrified.

Luckily, as I was being taken to the cell, a man who worked at the airport security office recognized me from TV. He told the police who I was and that they had the wrong guy. Thank God they believed him or I don't know what would have happened to me. I would probably still be rotting in prison over there right now. Later I found out that there was another guy, a doctor, with the same name as me, who had killed dozens and dozens of Baathists in Baghdad. When they saw my passport, they figured that it was me and that I was trying to flee the country. After we got it all straightened out, they put me in an army jeep with a bunch of commandos who took me out to my plane on the runway. They told the pilot what was going on, and I was then free to go. After that I knew I was making the right decision to leave. Needless to say, I drank a lot of champagne on that flight—I deserved it.

There was another guy, a doctor, with the same name as me, who had killed dozens and dozens of Baathists in Baghdad. When they saw my passport, they figured that it was me and that I was trying to flee the country.

When I finally got back to the States I ended up living all over the place, even out of the country. In fact, over the seven years after my return, I lived in Dallas, San Francisco, Portland, Honolulu, Australia, Japan, and London. I took advantage of the fact that I was single and made a good living traveling as a pro wrestler. The only downside was that I really couldn't ever spend more than six months to a year in any one spot. The promoters were always bringing in and shipping out new talent. That was the nature of the beast. If you got hot and the crowd liked you, you stayed. But if you weren't so popular, you would do your act and then head off to another territory. Back then there were about two dozen regional territories that fell under the NWA. So I spent the next several years traveling into and out of many of those territories, still working as Chief Billy White Wolf.

The one place where I finally settled down was Hawaii. I rented an apartment there and really enjoyed the climate. A lot of wrestlers lived there because it was halfway between the United States and the Far East. Plus, you couldn't beat all the beautiful girls there. Nothing was better than coming home from a long trip to Japan or somewhere and relaxing by the beach, and there were plenty of things there to keep you busy. Once I even costarred alongside Jack Lord on an episode of the TV show *Hawaii Five-0*. I was cast as a villain—it was perfect.

I will never forget another time in Hawaii when I met a gorgeous brunette while sun tanning at the Ilikai. We started talking, one thing led to another, and I was just about to ask her if she wanted to have dinner with me that night when this guy showed up. It was her husband—Elvis Presley! I was so embarrassed; I couldn't find a rock big enough to crawl under. Oh well, you live and you learn.

Because I had an apartment in Hawaii, a lot of other wrestlers would come over and stay with me. It was fun. One of my favorite roommates was Nick Bockwinkel, who went on to become the American Wrestling Association World Heavyweight Champion for nearly a decade. We did some wrestling there on the islands as well. I held the Hawaiian Heavyweight Championship several times during my years there and had a lot of fun with those crowds. In fact, one of my first tag-team partners there was a local guy by the name of Rocky

Johnson, whose son, Duane, is also known as "the Rock," the famous professional wrestler who is now a big Hollywood movie star. There were so many other great people who supported me while I was in Hawaii, such as Bob Rustigan, who really took me under his wing. Bob was an Armenian who had ties to the Middle East, and we really hit it off. He worked for a wealthy Chinese businessman in Hawaii and was able to show me the ropes. I was very grateful to him. He was like a brother to me.

> I was just about to ask her if she wanted to have dinner with me that night when this guy showed up. It was her husband —Elvis Presley!

While life on the road wasn't always terribly exciting, I will certainly never forget my time living in Texas back in 1963. My tag-team partner there was Harold Sakata, who had become famous for his role as "Odd Job" from the James Bond movie *Gold Finger*. One day we were on our way to a match, and we found ourselves right alongside the motorcade route of then-president John F. Kennedy. Not more than 20 seconds after waving at him as he drove by, we heard gun shots from the Texas School Book Depository Building. We actually witnessed his assassination; we saw history that changed the world. I was terrified. We were questioned, like everybody else there, and then let go. That is an image that I will take with me to my grave—I will never forget it. To be so young and to have seen two presidents get assassinated was unbelievable. First President Qassim in Baghdad, and then this. I thought I had gotten away from that by coming to America, but I guess I was wrong.

In addition to my adventures in America, I had a lot in other countries as well, because over the ensuing years I traveled overseas a great deal. I spent nearly a year in Australia and New Zealand and even wore the Australian World Heavyweight Championship belt for a while. Then I moved on to Japan and had great success there, too. They loved my character and always made me feel welcome. I even wound up living in London, where a promoter talked me into creating a new character called "the Sheikh." In the act, I was featured as an eccentric Arabian oil tycoon of sorts, complete with belly dancers and a big sword. Being the Sheikh was pure entertainment. I was already a religious sheikh by virtue of my father's title, so to then act like a "Hollywood" sheikh was a lot of fun. I am very proud of my Iraqi heritage, and this was just another way for me to express myself. It wasn't dishonorable or anything like that; it was just an act in order for me to make a living. I had to do what I had to do in order to advance my career. And it became very popular in England as well as throughout Europe. The fans loved it. I liked it, too, because it gave me another persona to work with. I had been acting as an Indian for my entire career and was excited about doing something different.

After my adventures overseas, I became a U.S. citizen in 1967 and finally felt like I belonged. It was a wonderful feeling and something that I vowed never to take for granted. I later fell in love with a Mormon gal from Utah. I was hoping to settle down, but it didn't work out because of our different religious backgrounds. Her family just couldn't accept me, and that

"The Sheikh" in all his glory.

was hard to take. Her mom also didn't like the fact that I was a professional wrestler, so it was tough. I was really hurt after that and started to feel like my life was spinning out of control. I think that all of the travel combined with not having a stable home life had taken a toll on me. I missed my family and was starting to feel like a nomad just wandering aimlessly from city to city. I think the final straw came when I spoke to my brother and he told me that our sister had died of cancer. I had been gone so long I didn't even realize that she had been ill. You see, my sister didn't have a lot of money, so they didn't have a telephone; therefore it was difficult for us to stay in touch. She had seven kids and had a hard time finding the time to write letters, so we fell out of communication for a while. I felt very bad about her whole situation; she was a good person. Like it or not, I was going home again.

> I missed my family and was starting to feel like a nomad just wandering aimlessly from city to city.

53

9

A "Short" Visit Back Home to Baghdad

WHEN I CALLED MY BROTHER to tell him that I was coming home to see him, he was very happy. It was 1969, and I had not been home for nearly seven years. I felt guilty about that and wanted to make up for lost time. I think I was avoiding my siblings because of the situation with my parents' deaths. Whatever the reason, I was ready to go back and spend some quality time with them, relaxing and catching up on old times. My nieces and nephews were growing up so quickly, and I wanted to see them. After all, several of them didn't even know who I was.

I flew back to Baghdad and immediately felt like I was home again. It was great to be back. I stayed with my brother and really enjoyed seeing my family and friends. And it wasn't long after I got home that I started getting asked to do more television interviews. Again, they were interested in portraying me as a young Iraqi who had found success in America and abroad as a champion wrestler. Shortly after the television interviews, I was featured on the cover of *al-Thawra*, the main newspaper, and before long I was being recognized on the streets as a sort of "local boy does good." It was nice to get all that attention, and I was enjoying my time back home very much.

One day I got a call from a Baath Party vice president; he wanted me to come down to meet the president. (Incidentally, that vice president's daughter was the five of hearts in the now-infamous "deck of cards." Her name is Dr. Huda Salih Mahdi Ammash, an Iraqi bioweapons scientist who became known as "Mrs. Anthrax" during the Gulf War.) The vice president sent for me, and I went to meet with him at his office. He said he was very proud of me and that the president wanted to meet me. The media was all there and it was really an honor; I couldn't believe the reception I was getting back home. It was a lot to handle, actually. I was nervous about meeting with the president; I didn't know what to expect. Politics were new to me, and I was cautious about what I was getting myself into. I knew a lot of the younger politicians, however, because many of them were acquaintances of mine from when I was growing up. I knew that if I smiled and just relaxed that everything would be all right, and it was.

A few days later I got a call to go meet with my old boyhood friend, Saddam Hussein. He literally summoned me to

One of my many front-cover photos on a Baghdad newspaper, al-Thawra.

meet him. I couldn't believe it. I was really afraid, to tell you the truth. I had heard stories about him since I left, and I can assure you they were not good. I knew he was up to something, but I didn't know what. Saddam was sneaky like a snake and knew exactly what he was doing. Whenever he met with people he would take his gun and lay it next to him on the table, just to intimidate them. He even brought the gun to my meeting with him. He was a ruthless man.

We got together to have tea and talk about old times. When I got to his office his stepbrother, who was in charge of his security, greeted and frisked me. Saddam and I then hugged and said hello. "Adnan, you haven't changed a bit," he said. "You look great." I told him he looked good, too, and that he still looked like he was 18. We chatted for a while and then started talking about politics. I was amazed to learn about what he had been up to for the previous 10 years. He had participated in the failed assassination of General Abdel Karim Kasim in 1959. And before fleeing to Syria, Saddam was involved in a coup attempt to kill then-president Kasim and was even shot in the midst of all the chaos. (He still has the bullet in his leg to this very day. He used to show it off like a badge of honor.) After spending some time in Syria, he went to law school in Egypt.

> Whenever [Saddam] met with people he would take his gun and lay it next to him on the table, just to intimidate them. He even brought the gun to my meeting with him.

He returned home a few years later and quickly rose up through the ranks of the Baath Party. In 1964 he went to prison for attempting to overthrow a party official, and when he got out he was elected head of the national Baath Party. Then, a few years later, he took over as chairman of the powerful Revolutionary Command

Council (RCC), the top decision-making body of the state. He had really risen up through the ranks, just as I always thought he would. It was just a matter of time before he took over everything.

In addition to his political activities, Saddam had married his first cousin, Sajida, a school teacher, in 1963. (Marrying a cousin is an acceptable practice throughout the Middle East. One of the big reasons for this is to ensure that wealth stayed within the family bloodlines.) Her father was Saddam's uncle, Khairallah Talfah, who would later be appointed as my boss. Together Sajida and Saddam had two sons: Odai and Qusai. (Needless to say, we would all hear about how well those two turned out.) Saddam later remarried and had three daughters from that marriage.

After I heard all about what he had been up to, the conversation turned to an entirely different subject and he started to tell me how excited he was about me being a world champion wrestler and making Iraq proud. He said that he really enjoyed pro wrestling but had never seen it in person, only on television. He wanted me to bring it to Iraq as soon as possible so that everyone could enjoy it. I was to make the arrangements and he would make sure that I had any resources necessary to make it happen. I told him I was flattered, but that I was only in town visiting my brothers for a few months.

"Adnan," he said, "I am offering you the job of a lifetime. We are going to take care of you. You are going to make us proud. We are going to use you as an example of who a model citizen really is. We want to show the world that Iraqis can travel abroad, get an education, learn about different cultures, and then come home to have great success. So we are not asking you to stay and do this, we are expecting you to do this as your duty to Iraq."

When Saddam smiled at me and then very subtly adjusted his gun, I knew that this was truly an "offer I couldn't refuse." So I agreed to set up a match for him at al-Shaab Stadium, where soccer games were usually played. I figured it would be fun to be the world champion from Iraq and bring in some friends to put on some shows. What I didn't realize was just how popular it would become, or how quickly it all would happen. What I also didn't realize was that Saddam knew exactly what would happen. The guy was very smart. He was going to use me as a ruse to divert attention away from politics and onto something new and different: professional wrestling. He was going to give the people something much more interesting to focus on than the government and politics. He was going to give them Adnan Alkaissy: soon-to-be European Heavyweight Champion. What I thought was going to be a relaxing vacation back home was about to turn into an eight-year saga with Saddam Hussein, one of the most infamous dictators the world has ever known.

> "We are going to use you as an example of who a model citizen really is. . . . So we are not asking you to stay and do this, we are expecting you to do this as your duty to Iraq."
>
> —SADDAM HUSSEIN

10

The People's Champion

AFTER MY MEETING WITH SADDAM, I started coordinating the details for what would prove to be the biggest sporting event in the history of Iraq. I had been around enough promoters in my life to know what had to be done, so I got to it, planning the entire production. It was going to take a lot of hard work and a lot of people to pull it off. The first thing I needed, however, was a worthy opponent.

One of the first things I did was call an old wrestler friend of mine from Canada, George Gordienko. He was the reigning European Heavyweight Champion at the time and was a really tough guy. I told him that I was putting together a match in Baghdad and asked if he was interested in taking part in a historic event: the first pro wrestling match in Iraqi history. George and I had good chemistry together on the mat, and I knew that I could trust him. I told him that it was probably going to be like nothing he had ever done before and that it was imperative that he follow my lead at every turn. He agreed.

I then began promoting the event, spending the following six months handling the logistics. I traveled the countryside doing a publicity tour, speaking about the big match at elementary schools, universities, and town halls. I was on TV, the radio, and in the newspapers—I was everywhere. I told them that I was their champion and that I had been instructed by both Saddam Hussein and the president, Ahmed Hassan al-Bakr, to set up this match and to bring honor to Iraq. The excitement was building, and I could tell I was onto something really big. They gave me a car and my own security detail as well. It was incredible. I went to each of the 14 provinces to tell people about it, and the response was overwhelming. Along the way, I stayed at the best hotels and was treated like royalty.

I also met with the minister of youth to tell him what was going on, and he told me that nobody cared about professional wrestling and that I would be lucky to have 50 people show up. I ignored him; I knew that it was going to be a big success. My ass was on the line, so I couldn't afford to screw it up. I really didn't know what the consequences were for failure, but I sure as hell did not want to find out.

Finally, after months of preparations, the big match took place during the summer of 1969 at al-Shaab Stadium in downtown Baghdad. It was unlike anything I had ever seen before in my life. There were at least two hundred thousand people

Greeting the crowd before my big match; notice the TV tower watching my every move from above.

crammed into the stadium and about one hundred thousand more standing outside watching on closed-circuit television. Plus, Iraqis around the country were tuned in on a live television feed. It was one of the biggest events in the country's history. It was just unbelievable. It seemed that if you were to throw a handful of salt from the ring to the top of the stadium, not a grain would touch the floor—that is how crowded it was. Every dignitary and politician in Iraq was there, with all the top brass sitting in the front rows. As I look back, I realize that most of the guys who are in President Bush's infamous deck of cards were there, too. It is amazing to think about now.

I had been working out with heavy weights a lot prior to the match, so I looked very fit. I had also been training with a bunch of local amateur wrestlers, to keep on top of my game. George came in a few nights prior to the match, and I got him a nice hotel in Baghdad. We talked very briefly about what was going to happen in the ring, but we didn't rehearse or choreograph anything—it wasn't like that. He was a professional, I was a professional, and we both knew how to follow each other's leads to make a good match. He obviously knew I was going to win; that was just understood. In fact, he was so terrified of being lynched by the mob of people that he told me once we got into the ring I better not even fall down too hard or he might get killed. I tried not to laugh out loud . . . if only he knew how true that really was.

> He was so terrified of being lynched by the mob of people that he told me once we got into the ring I better not even fall down too hard or he might get killed. I tried not to laugh out loud . . . if only he knew how true that really was.

Just before the match started I was getting ready in my dressing room and my phone rang. It was Saddam, calling from his office. "*Abo Kahtan*, how are you feeling?" he asked. (*Abo Kahtan* means "my son." That was my nickname over there.) "Are you ready for your big match? We are all counting on you to bring honor to Iraq and to not let us down." I assured him that I was well prepared and ready for this epic challenge. I told him I would not disappoint him and that in the end all of Iraq would be very proud. "Good. I am coming down to the match right now," he said. "That is great Abu-Odai [Abu-Odai was his nickname and later the name of his first son], we will wait to start the show until you get here," I replied.

By then the crowd was going nuts. They were chanting and wanted the match to start. But I could not start until Saddam got there—I wouldn't take that risk. So we waited. Finally I got word in my dressing room that Saddam was at the stadium but could not physically get down to the front row to sit with the dignitaries. It was just too packed with people, and they were worried about his safety. The decision was made that he would just sit in the general admission seats with his military guards surrounding him, so that he could at least witness the event first hand. The people who made that decision, by the way, were all fired by Saddam after that.

The match finally got underway after a bunch of ceremonial introductions. We locked up in the center of the ring and the crowd roared. It was so loud that I couldn't hear myself think. The people thought it was real, and that put a lot of pressure on me to make sure it looked perfect. If they sensed even for a moment that it wasn't legit, we both might not have made it out of the ring alive.

Things were going well, and there was a lot of back and forth action that the crowd really enjoyed. We didn't have a set

Going toe-to-toe with George Gordienko.

time limit, so we just sort of agreed that we would go until we were too tired to go anymore. It was a best-of-three-falls match, with George getting disqualified in the first match. We thought about him winning the second one, which is pretty typical, to set up a dramatic third and final contest, but we were too afraid that a riot might ensue if he beat me. So I won the second match by pinning him on a dramatic elbow drop (my signature finishing move) that knocked him senseless. We didn't want to take any chances, so with that, the referee raised my hand in victory and the crowd cheered like crazy.

The fans then began screaming and shooting their guns up in the air—it was like nothing I had ever seen before. (Shooting guns in the air is a typical form of celebration in Iraqi culture,

My first match ever in Baghdad against Canadian Heavyweight Champion George Gordienko.

Celebrating in the ring after the match at al-Shaab Stadium.

especially at weddings.) Thousands and thousands of people were firing their guns, and I was worried that someone was going to get shot. I mean after a while it got so smoky that you couldn't see a thing. Poor George was trying to duck down out of the way; he was terrified. After the celebration died down a little bit, I was presented with the European Heavyweight Championship belt. It was truly one of the greatest moments of my life. Hundreds of thousands of proud Iraqis were cheering for me because I was their champion.

The happiness didn't last for long though. After the match was over and the people were trying to get out, tragedy struck. Some bleachers that had been set up in the middle of the field collapsed. They were probably designed to seat five thousand people, but more like fifteen thousand people were piled on them. As a result, they buckled under the weight, and sadly, four people died. Many more were injured, and before long it was pandemonium. People started screaming and hollering, but nothing could be done because there were too many people there. They literally couldn't move; they were like sardines packed in a can. There was no way an ambulance could get in either. It was so scary. Meanwhile, I was watching all of this from up in the ring and couldn't believe my eyes. It looked like an escalator going down with all of the people falling on top of each other at the end.

Finally, I started wondering how I was going to get out of the stadium. Luckily, about 20 army commandos with machine guns came to get me. They surrounded me and just started moving out. Anybody in their way got smacked in the head with the butts of the commandos' guns. People were coming up to me to congratulate me and shake my hand, but the commandos were ordered to keep me safe, so they just started whacking people as they came up. It was surreal. As we approached the scene of the bleacher collapse I saw blood every-where. People were missing arms and legs; it was horrible. I felt so sad, but there was nothing I could do. And even in the midst of all the chaos, people were coming up to me and crying, because they just wanted to touch me and tell me that they loved me and were so proud of me. I was shocked. I had had moderate success in America and made a decent living, but now I was like a rock star, like royalty.

From there, the people poured out into the streets to celebrate. They were chanting "Kaissy, Kaissy, Kaissy"—it was unbelievable. As for George, I have no idea how he made it out. I am sure some security guards escorted him back to his hotel, but I am not sure how he was able to do it. As soon as I raised my hand in victory, all bets were off and it was every man for himself in there. Once the people rushed the ring, I lost track of everything. After that, the television crews hounded me, and I was thrust into the limelight as a national hero. I couldn't believe it.

Saddam was so happy. He really had no idea it was all fixed. If he had, I am pretty sure I would have been shot to death

> Even in the midst of all the chaos, people were coming up to me and crying, because they just wanted to touch me and tell me that they loved me and were so proud of me. . . . I was like a rock star, like royalty.

right there. Saddam became such a fan of it all that later, if anyone questioned whether or not it was real, he would just throw them in prison. He took it as a personal insult. After a while, professional wrestling became sacred. If Saddam liked it and believed it, then everybody did the same. I wasn't complaining—hey, I was his guy. And if you are Saddam's guy, you get perks . . . big perks. I know now that I could have asked for just about anything and gotten it—cars, money, riches—it was all right at my fingertips. But for Saddam the victory had a different significance: it represented a big victory for the Baath Party. The wheels of his master plan were then in motion. And as part of that plan, Saddam even said on television right after the match that my victory was just like the struggles of the Baath Party. He was very proud of my win and made sure to tell the country how significant it was.

> Saddam became such a fan of it all that later, if anyone questioned whether or not it was real, he would just throw them in prison.

Apparently the president, who was watching the match on television back at his palace, got so excited about the victory that when he jumped up and down he broke his TV. One of his guards later told me that he was so worked up that they swore he was going to have a heart attack right there in his office.

A few hours after the match, I contacted George and was relieved to hear that he had somehow made it back to his hotel. Meanwhile, I had to go to the hospital because I had gotten hit in the eye during the match and it had gotten so swollen that I couldn't see out of it. The next day President al-Bakr summoned both George and me to appear on live television. Because of the injury I had a huge bandage over my eye for my interview with the president. I told him that I got hit in the eye when a group of fans swarmed me afterward, because I didn't want anything bad to happen to George. I figured it was better to be safe than sorry. The president then told me on live TV that he and Iraq were very proud of me. He said, "You are now my *Ibne* [which means "son" in Arabic], and I will treat you as such. I am going to reward you with a big house, anywhere you want to build it, and a new Mercedes as a gift." I then said, "Thank you Mr. President for giving me this new home as a place to live in, and I want you to know that you will always live with me in my heart." He really liked that, and to be honest, I couldn't believe that I came up with something so articulate right on the spot like that. But he was a classy man, and I thought a lot of him.

11

A "Giant" Change in Lifestyle

BY THEN I WAS ON CLOUD NINE. There I was, a champion wrestler about to get my own house and Mercedes. It was as if I had won the lottery. I was moved out of my brother's house and into the penthouse at the luxurious Sahara Hotel in downtown Baghdad. Construction began on my house shortly after that, and about eight months later I moved to al-Mansoor, a very upscale area of Baghdad near the palaces along the Tigris River. The house had several big bedrooms, a gated entry, big gardens, the whole works—it was like a palace itself.

But while I was living at the Sahara Hotel waiting for construction on my place to be completed, I felt like a member of the Beatles. I couldn't even leave my room because, I swear to you, there were as many as five thousand people just sitting and waiting in front of the hotel to see me whenever I came and went. At first I thought it was wonderful, and then I hated it. I couldn't do anything without everybody wanting to be in my business.

As far as women went, that was difficult to deal with as well. Dating was very uncomfortable. In the Islamic culture, women cannot just come over to your house for drinks and that sort of thing. That type of behavior was simply not tolerated. It was much, much different. Women were not allowed to be alone with men unless they were family members. And the women could be punished severely if caught. So, if you wanted to go out and fool around you had to be really smart about it. You had to go out really late at night and not be seen. There were prostitutes out there, particularly at hotel bars, but that was not for me. Some people even went to Kuwait to visit brothels and many others had mistresses. I stayed clean and remained very disciplined. I had a girlfriend in London whom I would see from time to time when I went there on business or vacation. It was almost impossible for me to date anybody when I was in Iraq, so I just stuck with her. When I went to visit her in

> I felt like a member of the Beatles. I couldn't even leave my room, because, I swear to you, there were as many as five thousand people just sitting and waiting in front of the hotel to see me whenever I came and went.

London I could stay with her, but when she came to visit me in Baghdad, she stayed with my brother's family. You had to be very respectful of that sort of thing; in Middle Eastern culture dating is a different matter altogether. And I respected that, because I felt like I needed to be a model citizen, and that is how I chose to live my life.

Later, President Ahmed Hassan al-Bakr inquired to a colleague of mine about whether or not I might be interested in marrying his daughter. The president had three daughters; two of them were married, but the youngest one was not. Apparently, she saw me on television while I was wrestling and fell in love with me. The president liked me and thought I was worthy of her. But I wasn't ready for marriage at that point, so I had to explain to him that it just wasn't meant to be. But I was honored to be considered that type of person. The president was OK with my decision, but his daughter was very hurt. To be honest, there were many women who wanted my hand in marriage at the time, but I was simply not interested in settling down. And I particularly did not want to get involved with the daughter of a politician, because that would have meant that I was political—and I didn't want to have that type of association.

My popularity in Iraq was probably bigger than anybody's in the country at that point. I am not saying that to be boastful, it is just the truth. Even the poorest people knew who I was. While I was living at the hotel, fans would bring me gifts of money, clothing, and jewelry; they would ask me to bless them; and many others begged me to marry their daughters. Several people even brought me goats and sheep so that I could sacrifice them in honor of winning my match. When they did

The young champion—oh, those were the days!

that I would butcher the animals and then distribute the meat to the poor people. It got to be crazy. I finally had to have a guard battalion to protect me whenever I left the hotel.

Once I went into a store in Baghdad and so many people followed me, literally thousands, that traffic came to a complete stop in the city. It was a huge traffic jam and people were going nuts. I mean when people heard I was in this store they jumped out of their cars to see me, leaving their cars running. It was insane. What was so funny about it was that apparently Saddam and the president were on their way to a very important meeting at the time and got stuck in the traffic. He thought it was a coup, a revolution against the Baath Party. He had never seen anything like it, so he ordered the military out to see what the hell was going on. When they realized that it was me who was causing all the problems, they sent some commandos over to escort me out the back door of the store. Afterward I told Saddam that I was sorry and that I had just wanted to go out to buy a new pair of shoes. He said, "Adnan, we will buy you anything you want, just tell us. But please, please don't go out in public like that any more—it is very bad for the economy!"

People thought I was living like a king up in that penthouse, but in reality I felt like a prisoner. If I wanted to meet with someone or do anything I would have to wait until the middle of the night. Sometimes I would go out wearing a disguise so that I could just go to the market. It was the price to pay for fame, I suppose. I couldn't really date anybody either, which was very difficult after being so free to do so in America. You can't just run around and be carefree in Iraq. The Islamic culture is very different, and that type of behavior is simply unacceptable. So I hung out with my close friends and family a lot and we drank tea and ate nice meals. Even then, anyone who wanted to see me had to go through security that Saddam had set up in the hotel lobby. He was protecting me and building me up at the same time. He had a plan for the future and, unbeknownst to me, I was a big part of it. After

> Once I went into a store in Baghdad and so many people followed me, literally thousands, that traffic came to a complete stop in the city. . . . [Saddam] thought it was a coup.

My identification card as the general director of youth at the Ministry of Youth.

about a year or so I knew what was going on with Saddam. I knew that he was using me for his own personal interests, but I didn't care because I was achieving a lot for myself at the same time. I had become rich and famous beyond my wildest dreams. I just focused on making money and having a good time at my job. The political things were out of my control.

One day I was meeting with an old high school friend of mine who was the minister of foreign affairs. I was in his office getting a VIP passport, which allowed me to have nearly unlimited access throughout the country. While we were visiting Saddam walked in. "Adnan," he said, "how are you doing?" We kissed each other and sat down to visit. I told him things were going well and that I was very honored to have the opportunity to represent my country as its champion. He told me that they put me on a pedestal as someone who was a good athlete, a good person, and a true gentleman. He said that he and the president were proud of me and that they were going to reward my hard work. He then picked up the phone and called the Revolutionary Command Council to inform them that Adnan Alkaissy was going to be the new general director of youth at the Ministry of Youth. I couldn't believe my ears. This was an incredible position, and it was given to me just like that. I was so excited that I nearly hit the ceiling. That was one of the best jobs someone like myself could get.

In my new position I would be in charge of youth athletics, which was something I really loved. I would be able to help kids learn about sports and then help them to participate in their neighborhoods. I would be setting up soccer fields, swimming pools, and youth recreation centers and organizing leagues for the kids to play in throughout the entire country. Iraq had built up a network of several hundred community centers, and I was going to be involved in making sure that they were available to the children. In addition, I would be able to talk to kids about the dangers of drugs, smoking, and alcohol and the virtues of hard work.

The job was just a perk for my hard work and for bringing honor to my country. It meant a great salary, a car, and a lot of stability. You never knew what was going to happen with regards to getting injured in the ring, so this was a nice insurance policy that I could have for the future. The next day I posed for a picture with Saddam as he was appointing me to my new position, and it appeared on the front cover of *al-Thawra*, the national newspaper. It was a dream job.

Meanwhile, Saddam had instructed me to line up a second match. So I set up a rematch with George Gordienko in the southern port city of Basra, Iraq. It was a huge match with a lot of people in attendance from all over the area, including Kuwait. We got George his own Mercedes complete with a driver and security detail. It was a big deal, and there was a lot of media coverage over the event. George and I went three rounds in this match, too, which was quite different from our previous match. He was terrified to win one of the rounds because he didn't know what the fans were going to do to him if he beat me, but it all worked out. I lost the round as the result of a disqualification—he didn't pin me. I remember when the referee came over to raise his hand, George told him to get away from him. It was pretty funny. I had to hold my breath from laughing. After I won there was a huge celebration in the streets of Basra. This was their first match ever in the city, and the people there were really excited. Although we did pack another soccer stadium and deemed it a big success, it was nothing like the first match.

> I lost the round as the result of a disqualification—he didn't pin me. I remember when the referee came over to raise his hand, George told him to get away from him.

Disappointed with this second match, Saddam told me to make the third one the biggest yet. In fact, I was instructed to put on the biggest athletic spectacle of all time. And incredibly, that is exactly what I did. I will never forget it. It was January 1971 and I had spent months preparing for the next big match back at al-Shaab Stadium. To make sure this one would be even

Being congratulated by an Iraqi general after a match.

bigger and better, I brought in the 7'4", 500-pound French behemoth Andre the Giant. He was just massive, but he was also a tremendous athlete and as strong as an ox. People didn't even believe that there could be somebody that big when I first announced that he would be my next opponent. I had met him when I was wrestling in England and asked him if he wanted to come over. He agreed, "as long as there was plenty of good food." I told him we would treat him like a king, and we did.

81

It was the 50th anniversary celebration of the Iraqi Army, and my title bout against the Giant was to be the focal point of the festivities surrounding the big event. It was a huge deal. There were parades, parties, the whole nine yards. Normally, Iraqis refer to the holiday as Army Day, but this time the bicentennial was really hyped up like never before. Foreign dignitaries from around the world were even brought in, and the government spared no expense in putting on a great show. It was only fitting that I was able to bring in the biggest man in the world for the biggest show of my life.

> They were so in awe of [Andre the Giant's] feet that they made an extra pair of his size 24 shoes to display in their front window. People lined up for blocks to see them, and the shoes remained in the window for years.

I brought Andre in about a week before the event, and we planned the match and did some promotional stuff. People were just in awe of the guy. I put him up at the Sahara Hotel, and they had to have a bed custom made for him. I got a really big Mercedes for him, too, along with four armed guards—we really did it up right. He couldn't believe it. I remember he went shopping one day and wound up having a pair of shoes custom made at this ritzy shoe store in downtown Baghdad, the Bata Shoe Company. They were so in awe of the guy's feet that they made an extra pair of his size 24 shoes to display in their front window. People lined up for

A group of prominent Baath Party officials led by the vice president (middle of photo in suit) coming to my match.

blocks to see them, and the shoes remained in the window for years.

Andre, who was French, loved to eat fine foods from around the world. And, at over 500 pounds, he could really put it away. The guy had an appetite like a horse's. It was not uncommon for him to put away several meals in one sitting, followed by either a 12-pack of beer or an entire bottle of brandy. Thousands of people followed him around all week; it was like having a giant walking billboard advertise our match—it was great. Some people just wanted to see him in person, because he was like a freak show. Other people were terrified of him and ran away crying. It was something else. We also toured around the country together for a day to promote the match. We even went to a luncheon put on by the Iraqi minister of defense at the Iraqi Military Academy. The cadets couldn't believe their eyes. They thought I was the biggest guy they had ever seen—and whoa!—this guy was twice my size. It was unbelievable to them.

Finally, the big day of the match came and there was electricity in the air. In all, there were more than three hundred thousand fans crowded in and outside al-Shaab Stadium to watch the festivities—even more people than at the first match. Those outside the stadium were watching on closed circuit TV. And, because of the anniversary celebration, the stadium was filled with tens of thousands of Iraqi soldiers—all with their Kalashnikov rifles. It was a sea of green uniforms as far as my eyes could see. It was really quite a sight. Foreign leaders from as far away as the United States, Germany, Japan, Korea, Russia, England, as well as all of the Arab countries from around the Middle East were there to help us celebrate. To commemorate their arrivals, Iraqi Television was broadcasting live from the airport as they landed. Things were very tense and the powers that be were intent on making sure that nothing went wrong.

About 15 minutes before the opening ceremonies, Mohammed Saeed al-Sahaf, the manager of the television station, decided to switch coverage from the parade of dignitaries to al-Shaab Stadium. But when some high-ranking members of the Baath Party saw that the station had switched over and was no longer covering the parade, they notified the president. When the president realized that the parade was not being televised, he immediately figured that a coup was

Greeting a group of dignitaries before a match, including the vice president (middle) and Izzat al-Doori (far left), Saddam's right-hand man.

taking place. So he panicked and started contacting his top generals to prepare for battle. Remember, these guys were very paranoid about being overthrown, and with all of the festivities going on this would have been a prime opportunity to do something. Usually, when a coup does happen, the first thing that is taken over is the national television station so that the revolutionaries can control the media. Luckily, someone told him what had happened and that everything was all right. He was so upset, though, that he sent word to fire the television manager immediately.

Meanwhile, back at al-Shaab Stadium, Andre and I were getting ready to go out. I was really nervous. As I entered the

85

Here I am at the 50th anniversary celebration of the Iraqi Army doing battle with Andre the Giant at al-Shaab Stadium.

ring I mingled with the delegates in the front rows, shook some hands, and took some pictures. I said hello to the president, and then went over to Saddam. He then whispered into my ear, "Be victorious, Adnan, we are all counting on you. Be victorious.

This guy is big, but he is a pussy. I know that you can beat him. If he hurts you in any way, he is going to get this. [He lifted up his coat to show me a solid gold pistol.] I will put every bullet in there in his fat head and send him back to France in a pine box."

To say I was scared at that point would be a gross understatement. But I just smiled and nodded. Remember, Saddam thought this was all real. He also told me that Iraq was counting on me to win and that I had better not let down the country or the people on such a special day. He didn't actually threaten me, but the way he looked at me I knew that if I didn't win I was going to be in big trouble. I just prayed to God that Andre didn't fall on me or something and hurt me. Little did he know but a fall like that could wind up being deadly—for both of us.

Andre and I finally entered the ring, and after shaking hands, we got down to business for a best-of-three-falls match with the winner taking home the newly created Arab World Championship belt. We locked arms at the center of the ring, and the crowd went absolutely crazy. They were chanting

> [Saddam] then whispered into my ear, "Be victorious, Adnan, we are all counting on you. . . . This guy is big, but he is a pussy. . . . If he hurts you in any way, he is going to get this. [He lifted up his coat to show me a solid gold pistol.]"

"Adnan, Adnan, Adnan," and I could barely hear myself think it was so loud. Andre and I had rehearsed a little bit of what we were going to do, and luckily everything went off without a problem. I even body slammed him in the ring, and I thought the crowd was going to riot at that point. It was really a thrill. Of course, Andre helped me out, as all good pro wrestlers are trained to do, and we made it look like the real thing. He even bounced off the mat, which totally sold the move to the crowd. They were convinced that I could press 500 pounds over my head just like that—it was great.

As for the dramatic finish? Well, after Saddam gave me his "uplifting" little pep talk, I had to change the ending. Because it was a best-of-three-falls match, I was going to have Andre beat me in the second fall so that I could win the third one in dramatic fashion. But I didn't know what Saddam might do if Andre beat me, so I had to tell him about my change of plans while we were in the ring. It was tough to do, but when we got into a headlock position I whispered it to him in his ear and he nodded OK. I prayed that he heard me all right, because I did not want that big SOB pinning me out there and then getting shot to death right on top of me.

I won the first fall and then took the second to win the match. I again used my signature elbow drop to finish him off. When they raised my hand in victory and put the new shiny belt on me, the crowd went ballistic. And, just like the last time, they all started shooting their guns up into the air to celebrate. Andre, meanwhile, couldn't believe his eyes. He was terrified and just lay down on the mat. He didn't know if they were shooting at him or not. He was nearly in tears he was so scared. Finally, a bunch of the dignitaries jumped up into the ring to hug me

Upending Andre the Giant at al-Shaab Stadium.

and shake my hand. They shook Andre's hand, too, and told him that he should train harder and maybe lose a few pounds if he wanted to have a successful career as a wrestler. Boy, if they only knew.

Afterward, we took pictures together, did some television interviews, and ate like pigs. It was great. Later, when I got home, I got a call from Mohammed Saeed al-Sahaf, the television station manager who had been fired for his decision to

Being congratulated by the head of Saddam's security detail, Dawoud al-Janabi.

cut away from the parade early and go live at the stadium instead. He was crying and very upset. He told me he felt awful about what he did and asked me if I could please help him get his job back. I felt terrible that he lost his job on account of me, and I wanted to make it right. So I got in my car and drove over to see President al-Bakr personally, and I asked him to please reconsider giving al-Sahaf his job back. I tried to take the blame for some of it by saying that he needed extra time to get his equipment set up at the stadium. I asked for his forgiveness and to spare the man his dignity. The president said that he was proud of me and if it was that important to me then it would be done immediately. I promised him another incident like that would never happen again and then kissed and thanked him.

> The match with Andre was so successful in Baghdad that about a week later he and I wrestled again in the city of Kuit, near Fallujah.

What is so amazing about this story is that although most Americans probably don't recognize the name Mohammed Saeed al-Sahaf, they do know the name "Baghdad Bob." Well, that's the guy. He later became infamous as Saddam's minister of information during Operation Iraqi Freedom. The media had a field day with this guy when the U.S.-led coalition forces were invading Baghdad. He was on every TV station around the world telling viewers that there were "no American tanks in Baghdad" as American tanks were rolling through the streets behind him. It was unbelievable. My

The big rematch with Andre the Giant in the central Iraqi province of Kuit.

friends later teased me and said that even though I was retired from wrestling, I was still providing quality entertainment on TV. I had to agree.

The match with Andre was so successful in Baghdad that about a week later he and I wrestled again in the city of Kuit,

92

near Fallujah. I convinced him to stick around and promised him that he didn't have to worry about getting shot after our match this time. He laughed, but made me promise him a lot of good food and wine in return. I think the $10,000 paycheck might have had something to do with him agreeing to a rematch, too. That was big bucks in those days. The turnout for the second match was good, but nothing like the one at al-Shaab Stadium. We had a really good show though, and I, of course, won again.

Incidentally, there's a really good story about our rematch that I didn't hear until many years later. Apparently a pregnant woman was watching the match on TV, and when Andre body slammed me, she got so upset that she went into labor and delivered her child right there on her living room floor. Appropriately, she named her new son Adnan, in my honor. Of course, I had no knowledge of this when it happened, but about 15 years later I was in Abu Dhabi (the United Arab Emirates) for a match. I had since moved back to America, but was wrestling in the Middle East as part of a touring promotion. I was killing time one afternoon before a match, and I stumbled upon a beautiful store called Adnan's Jewelry. Adnan

> I picked a beautiful solid-gold chain of worry beads. And do you know what? To this day I still rub them and think of my family back home. It is one of my most prized possessions, and it truly brings back fond memories of my days in Iraq.

was not that popular of a name, so I thought I would go in and check it out. I figured, "Hey, maybe they will offer me a discount because my name is Adnan, too." I walked in and immediately this young man behind the counter frantically asked me if I was Adnan Alkaissy. I said, "Yes. Do I know you?" He then ran down to the basement screaming, "Mom, Dad, come quick, you will never guess who is in the store—it is him! Adnan is here!" He then came rushing back up with his parents and they all started kissing me and telling me that it was God's fate that I had finally arrived there. He then told me his amazing story about his mother naming him after me during that match with Andre so many years earlier. I couldn't believe my ears. They said they were such big fans that after they moved away from Iraq (to the UAE) they even named their store after me. I couldn't believe it.

We visited for a while, took some pictures, and had a really nice time. Then, just as I was about to leave, he told me that I could choose any item in the store that I wanted, as a gift. I said no thank you, but he insisted. So I picked a beautiful solid-gold chain of worry beads. And do you know what? To this day I still rub them and think of my family back home. It is one of my most prized possessions, and it truly brings back fond memories of my days in Iraq.

12

Settling In

AFTER THE REMATCH WITH **ANDRE,** I settled into a groove where I did about two big matches a year. From a business perspective, I had a monopoly on professional wrestling. I was the only professional wrestler in Iraq, and really throughout most of the Middle East. I had to bring in all of my competition from either Europe or America. The guys I brought in loved it because I paid them more than they would make anywhere else, and the locals loved it because it gave the whole thing an international flavor.

I never lost a match in Iraq, either. I was untouchable, and everybody who came in to wrestle me knew what the outcome was going to be. It was a job to them, and as long as the check didn't bounce, they didn't care. Believe me, they did not want to win, because they knew if they did they might be

Meeting and greeting the European Heavyweight contenders at the Baghdad Airport for an upcoming tournament.

shot dead right there in the ring. Sure, sometimes I lost a fall, when it was a best-of-three-falls match, but only to make the third and final fall more dramatic. And when I lost these falls,

The vice president raising my hand in victory at al-Shaab Stadium.

96

it was always by a disqualification from the referee—never from being pinned by my opponent. It was a good gig, that was for sure.

My next big match was back at al-Shaab Stadium against an American Heavyweight Champion by the name of Bob Roop. Bob and I had wrestled back in the States, and I thought we would have a good match together. So I brought him and his very pretty fiancée, Debbie, in and put them up in a nice hotel, complete with their own security guards.

Later, at the match, Bob and I were getting ready to square off in the ring and everything was going smoothly; Debbie was sitting ringside and appeared to be enjoying herself when I looked over at her. Then, as the match went on, the crowd started to really get into it. Pretty soon some really wild fans began rushing toward the ring to cheer me on. The army commandos, who were positioned at ringside, then started beating them back with the butts of their rifles. With two hundred thousand fans in the stadium, the security had to be

Here I am grappling with Bob Roop in front of more than two hundred thousand fans at al-Shaab Stadium.

tight in order to prevent a riot. By then the commandos were ordering everybody back to their seats. But the fans didn't care, they kept coming. At that point the commandos really started whacking the fans, and blood was everywhere. Poor little Debbie got so freaked out that she got sick and fainted right there in her seat. I just happened to see it out of the corner of my eye, so I kept Bob facing the other direction. A few moments later, Bob and I locked up in the corner and he whispered to me that he couldn't see Debbie and was really afraid. He was shaking like a leaf. I told him to relax and that I saw her go with a guard to the bathroom. What he didn't realize was that about a half dozen commandos had already picked her up and carried her through the crowd to an awaiting ambulance.

We finished our match and afterward I told Bob what had happened and that she was safe. I said, "I couldn't tell you at the time because I was worried you would panic and we would ruin the match. If that happened and it looked fixed, then we both might not get out alive." He thanked me and agreed that he probably would have done exactly that.

After the match was over the fans started shooting their guns in the air and poor Bob hit the deck to take cover. Then, when the referee raised my hand in victory, I wanted to show the fans that I was a good sport, so I signaled to Bob that I wanted to raise his hand, too, and thank him for coming all the way from America to challenge me. I grabbed his hand and he whispered, "Damn it, Adnan, put my hand down! I don't want these people to mistakenly think that I won . . . they might kill me!" Looking back, I think he was probably right. We both laughed after that one, knowing we narrowly dodged a big bullet.

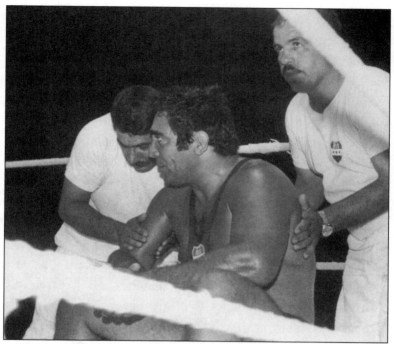

Taking a much-deserved timeout between falls during a best-of-three match at al-Shaab Stadium.

After that match life was good. I was enjoying living in my new home. I also had a new Mercedes with a chauffeur and a bodyguard. However, I was still being hounded by fans who wanted to talk to me and just be around me. I never got used to that; it was very bizarre. I felt like Elvis sometimes, not having a normal life. But my job at the Ministry of Youth was going very well. I would go into the office for an hour or two a day, depending on how much work I had to do promoting wrestling matches. One of the toughest parts about my job, however, was the fact that so many people wanted me to do favors for them. It got to be too much. I was helping so many people with their problems that I could barely do my own job, but those are stories for another chapter.

I had a very good job though, and probably made about $500 per month, which was an outstanding salary back then. I was even making a lot more than my brother, who was a judge. The big bucks came in the ring though. I was making so much money putting on wrestling matches that I literally couldn't spend it fast enough. I was making a killing. The match with George Gordienko alone netted about $1 million, and the one with Andre made even more. As the promoter, I set it all up: I charged $10 to $15 per ticket for the matches, and after I paid all the expenses I was making a fortune. Saddam didn't care how much money I was making; he just wanted to make sure that I won the matches and that Iraq was being well represented. As I've said before, he had much bigger plans in his future, and my success meant that the people would have something to think about other than politics. He knew I was making money, but he just let me be. And the government made a bunch of money when they made my matches into reel-to-reel movies, which they sold and played at local movie theaters. I couldn't touch that money.

I remember one time my cousin came over to my house to help me with my finances. It is so funny to think back about it now, but I had several huge suitcases filled with cash stuffed in my hall closet. We couldn't even close them they were so full of money. There were millions in there, but they were Iraqi dinars, not U.S. dollars, so I had to exchange them somehow. I knew that if I put the money in the bank the government would know how much I had, and then I might have had a problem taking it out if I needed it down the road. You see, the government didn't have a problem with me having money, but they did have a problem with me spending my money abroad. They wanted the money to stay in Iraq. I didn't know. I mean, what if I lost a match or something crazy happened? Saddam might fire me, too. Or worse. My goal was to get the money converted and then out of the country, but I didn't know how.

After a few years I had a couple million dollars in cash at my house and couldn't do a damn thing with it. So I used it to buy my brothers' and cousins' families really nice things. I just did whatever I could to help as many people as I could because I didn't know how long it was going to last. Eventually, I just put it in the bank, because I was afraid I would have a fire in my house or get robbed or something. It turned out that putting the money in the bank was a big mis-

> It is so funny to think back about it now, but I had several huge suitcases filled with cash stuffed in my hall closet. We couldn't even close them they were so full of money.

take. Later, Saddam realized how much I was making and, wanting to find a way to monitor my cash flow, appointed a committee headed by his father-in-law, Khairallah Talfah, who had become governor in 1970 when Saddam took charge of the RCC, to take over the business side of my matches. He figured his father-in-law would handle the operations and just leave the wrestling to me. Needless to say, that put an end to my cash-flow problems in a hurry.

Here I am in Baghdad about to give Cameron, a Scottish wrestler, an elbow drop.

After the committee started coordinating my matches, it became nearly impossible for me to make any money from them. I still had my salary from my job and was still being paid handsomely for participating in my matches, but I wasn't getting any additional cash as I had before. Instead, the government just gave me a sort of open line of credit. In addition to my house, car, and expenses, if I needed money for anything, all I had to do was ask. It wasn't uncommon for me to ask my committee leader for as much as $50,000 so that I could buy a new car or something. It was insane. They wouldn't even

Giving the Scottish wrestler Cameron a leg stomp.

think twice; they just gave it to me. I was helping the Baath Party big time. I was doing my part to give the common people something to cheer for and to take their minds off politics. It was great publicity for the party, and I was doing my part as an Iraqi citizen. I think they were so free with the money because I earned it—I was the one promoting my matches, and I was the one performing in the ring. And the fact that wrestling's popularity exploded in Iraq was really because of me. I was very proud of that.

13

The Price of Fame

LIFE ON TOP WAS GOOD, but there most certainly was
a price to pay for the lifestyle I was living. Sure, dealing with
fans and well-wishers was sometimes frustrating, but I was usually humbled and flattered by their attention. What was
extremely difficult to deal with, however, were people who
got jealous and then became spiteful.

One day my life was nearly changed forever. I got a call to
come into Governor Khairallah Talfah's office. He showed
me a letter that he had received in which an underage girl
accused me of raping her at her home. I couldn't believe it. I
was petrified. Of course it was a fabrication, and I could prove
it because I was actually in Kuwait during the time of the alleged
incident. So they sent a police car over to the girl's house and
brought her in for questioning. When they started asking her

Signing autographs with the governor at the shrine in Karballah.

about it, she broke down and said that it wasn't true and that four men came to her and made her sign the document saying that she had been raped. She said that they would kill her and her family if she did not do as they said. She gave the authorities enough information to figure out who the guys were, and they then went out and rounded up all four of them. Incredibly, when they came walking into the police station, I almost started to cry. I knew all four of them. I had helped them a great deal over the years: I had gotten them jobs as security officers during my matches and had even given them money to help them out when they needed it. They all confessed right then and there and said the reason they did it was because they were jealous of me. They resented me for my success and wanted to strike back at me.

From there, all four of them came over to me, crying, and started to kiss my shoes. They apologized and begged me for their mercy. I told them that I wanted nothing to do with them and that it was up to the authorities to decide what was going to happen to them. I said that they had tried to ruin my life, so I was not going to stand in the way of justice. They each got a couple of years in the infamous Abu Ghraib prison, and I didn't feel a bit guilty about it. They lost their jobs, got fined, and I am pretty sure they got beaten up pretty good, too. But I felt that they deserved it, because the allegations they made against me were very serious and would have ruined or cost me my life.

Another incident happened to me just prior to a big match in Baghdad. There was a high-ranking member of the Baath Party who had his own one-hour sports show on TV. One night just before my match, I was watching and I heard him jabbing

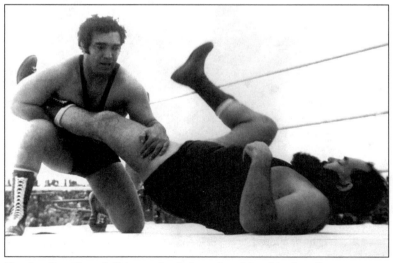

Putting Ian Campbell into a leg lock and making him beg for mercy.

107

Putting Ian Campbell, the Scottish Heavyweight Champion, into a chin lock.

Grappling with Ian Campbell, the Scottish Heavyweight Champion.

me pretty good. I couldn't believe my ears. He said, "Saturday night Adnan Alkaissy [he disrespected me by not saying that I was the champion] will take on the European Heavyweight Champion, Ian Campbell, from Scotland, and the outcome, I can tell you right now, will definitely be Alkaissy." He was really making a mockery out of the whole thing and basically insinuating that it was all fake. You didn't question that kind of thing back then. In fact, it was a big insult to not only me, but my superiors, too.

A couple of high-ranking members of the Baath Party saw the program and got really pissed off. They called me and asked me about it, and I told them that the guy was very jealous of me and was clearly trying to disrespect me on national TV. From there, they just went off on the guy: "That SOB! We got that guy his position in the party as well as on television, and here he is doing this to you and also to us. He is going to pay." They called the vice president and had the guy fired immediately from not only the TV show, but also his position with the Ministry of Youth. They later told the guy that he was going to be transferred down to the southern city of Basra, where he would be demoted to an elementary school teacher. It was a huge slap in the face.

I was out of town for a while after that, but when I got back I found the guy camped out at my house waiting for me. When I pulled in he came over to me and said he was sorry and that he would do anything to make it right. He really wanted to get his job back and was desperate. He said that someone else had told him to say those things on TV, and they threatened to punish him severely if he didn't. I asked him who did it, and he told me that it was a former amateur wrestler who had since moved to Germany and was a big shot in the Baath Party. He was very jealous of my success and wanted to take my World Heavyweight title belt from me.

When I told this to the vice president, he called the guy in for a meeting. There, he threatened him pretty good, saying, "If you open your mouth again you will never open your mouth again . . . because you will be dead." I could have just let it end there, but because I am such a nice guy and have a real problem doing things that are negative, I got the guy his television job back. It turned out to be a good move, though, because after that I was practically the star of his show. He was so grateful that he featured me as the lead story every week.

The final incident that I can recall regarding the price of fame came during the mid-seventies and it truly scared the hell out of me. There was a terrorist named Abu Tobar, nicknamed the "Axe Man," who had been killing prominent members of the Revolutionary Command Council. He was from a rival political group and was trying to terrorize everybody. Somehow this guy had already killed more than 50 people over about a four-month stretch, most of them politicians and dignitaries, as well as their families. One day I got a call from the governor and he told me that I was probably going to be the next victim on the psychopath's list. I said, "What! Why do you think this?" He told me that a panel studying this guy had met and felt that if the Axe Man could kill me, the people's champion, someone well liked and famous, that would strike a great deal of fear into the hearts of the Iraqi people. They would know that if Iraq's toughest man was murdered, anybody could be taken out, and that would hurt the country's morale.

He told me to watch out and that I should increase my security. He appointed a couple of extra security guards for me and gave my chauffeur a machine gun. He even told me that if I could catch this guy, the party would give me a $10 million reward. But they eventually caught the guy on their own, and when they did, they interrogated him and found out that he had actually been up on the roof of my house one day waiting for me to come home. Luckily, I had been away on business at the time or I

> There was a terrorist named Abu Tobar, nicknamed the "Axe Man," . . . One day I got a call from the governor and he told me that I was probably going to be the next victim on the psychopath's list.

would have been killed for sure. At first I was really shaken up when I heard this, but then I was just glad that it was over. And then I was sad: hey, what if I had been home that day and I had captured him with my elbow drop? Ten million bucks down the drain. Oh well, they executed the SOB and I was just happy that it was all over. I could finally sleep again.

14

The Diplomat Grappler

SADDAM EVENTUALLY SAW MY WRESTLING as not only a ruse to further his own interests, but also a foreign relations propaganda tool. He sent me out to meet with the presidents of nearly every Arab country with the intention of arranging wrestling matches in each of them. It was incredible how quickly they all agreed to matches. The other foreign leaders knew that Saddam was an up-and-coming force to be reckoned with, and they did not want to get on his bad side. So they said, "No problem," and I was able to set up matches all over the place. As a result, I was wined and dined by a lot of really important dignitaries from around the Middle East who wanted to make sure I was treated right. They knew that

Enjoying a match alongside the governor of Samawa (left) and a promi-nent Baath Party official with his son (right).

if they helped me out with my matches they would be in Saddam's good graces. Before long I was wrestling in front of packed stadiums throughout the entire Arab world and had become very popular outside of Iraq.

I became a sort of envoy, or diplomat, sent to establish new business and political ties throughout the region. Because I was a hero in the Arab world, Saddam used me as a messenger for him to make new contacts and sort of break the ice with other leaders. I remember one trip to the United Arab Emirates when, as a sort of goodwill ambassador, I went to a bunch of oil billionaires' palaces to say hello to their kids. These homes were unlike anything I had ever even dreamed of. They were so opulent—I couldn't believe my eyes. It was the finest of everything, from Rolls-Royces to Bentleys, to gold and diamonds everywhere. I came back from that trip with about a dozen gold Rolex watches as gifts. It was unbelievable. I was having a

Being wined and dined alongside the chief of police of Karballah (on my right), as well as some other Baath Party members.

great time, to tell you the truth—I was traveling around the Middle East as a celebrity. I was earning a living and working very hard. I did what I was told to do and didn't make any waves. Sure, I knew Saddam was rising to power, but in retrospect, I never could have imagined how brutal he would become years later. No one knew.

After I organized the matches, I got to travel to those countries and wrestle as the Arab Heavyweight Champion. The fans seemed to embrace me wherever I went, which always made my job easier. I once did a match in Kuwait City in front of about eighty thousand people. It was the biggest athletic event in the country's history. Muhammad Ali was even there, raising money for some Muslim causes back in America. I think he raised a couple million dollars in cash that night because all of the Arab leaders wanted him to build a mosque back in the States. He did a boxing exhibition before my match, and I got to meet him

Here I am in the Kurdish capital of Kirkuk along with the champs from Portugal, France, and Scotland.

Getting introduced in the ring and waving to the crowd before a big match in the central city of Kuit.

116

afterward. It was really interesting to talk to him. He was someone I greatly admired, so it was a real thrill to meet him.

It didn't take Saddam long to figure out that my matches were bringing in a lot of money. These foreign leaders had big bucks and weren't afraid to spend them on events like my matches. I can remember talking with Saddam about everything back at his office in Baghdad; he was really excited about it. I could tell that he was getting a lot of mileage out of all the publicity and was anxious to parlay that into political clout. It worked, too, because the leaders of the other Arab nations would all come visit him in Baghdad to kiss his ass. In fact, over the years I think I met nearly every one of the top leaders in the Middle East at one point or another: from Moammar Gadhafi to Yasser Arafat, to King Hussein of Jordan and President Idi Amin of Uganda, to the Saudi royal family and the emir of Kuwait. In fact, I even met former U.S. Secretary of Defense Donald Rumsfeld when he was a Middle East envoy in Iraq back in the early seventies. I had dealings with him on a couple of occasions; he was a very interesting guy. He told me that he was impressed with how popular I was. We used to talk about college wrestling because he

> I once did a match in Kuwait City in front of about eighty thousand people. It was the biggest athletic event in the country's history. Muhammad Ali was even there, raising money for some Muslim causes back in America.

Receiving a congratulatory pistol from the governor of Kirkuk.

Saddam and I doing an interview.

118

had been the captain of his Princeton University wrestling squad. It is remarkable to think that after he spent all of that time in Iraq, years later he was the one planning a war there.

I met all these people because I was invited to a lot of social functions with Saddam. He liked having me there because he could use me to keep the conversations light. He loved to talk about wrestling, and if I could divert the attention away from politics, that was all right by him. One time I was at this big annual Baath Party political function and just about every top-level member of the party was there. We were all talking and having a good time. Suddenly, Saddam came up behind me and grabbed me. He said, "Adnan, let's have some fun. Go over and tell the president that you want to accept his challenge to a match, right here in front of all these people." I told him that he was crazy, but he assured me that it would be a good joke. So I went over to the president and speaking really loudly I said, "Mr. President, thank you for having me at your party today; I am honored to be here. I would like to tell you that I have decided to accept your challenge to a 10-minute professional wrestling match. I have been told that you feel that you can beat me, and I think it would be appropriate for us to have this match right here, right now, in front of all of these dignitaries as witnesses."

Then I grabbed him and put him in a headlock. Everybody gasped. His eyes got really big, and he started begging me to put him down. He screamed that he would never challenge me like that and began yelling for help. It was hilarious. Saddam then started smiling, and the room erupted with laughter. I gently put him down and hugged him. Luckily he had a good sense of humor about it, because looking back I realize that I

At a dinner function alongside the chief of police of Karballah (left) and the European Wrestling Federation president George Relwyskow (right).

might have been shot if I had taken the prank too far. Afterward, the president grabbed me and then looked right at Saddam and said, "I know who put you up to this." I think those guys enjoyed having me around for stuff like that. I was never involved with political decisions, but they liked the fact that I could make certain situations more enjoyable. That was nice.

After being with Saddam on various occasions over the years, I came to the conclusion that the guy had eyes in the back of his head. It was nerve-racking being with him. He was so paranoid all the time, and it drove me nuts. If someone was supposed to meet with him and they were a few minutes late, he would just assume that there was a coup or a revolution going on.

Here I am with the governor of Samara (on my right), a province near Baghdad, along with several other Baath Party officials, out to visit some historic ruins.

But I remember one time when there actually was an attempted coup. I was at the airport as part of an official welcoming committee to greet the president, who was returning from an important meeting in Europe. Well, word came in that a coup was in fact in the works. Because the president was out of the country, the timing was perfect. Nadhim Kazzar, the head of Iraq's security service, was behind it, and it was big. He was a high-ranking member of the Baath Party and wanted to take over.

Saddam was very suspicious and paranoid. He didn't trust anybody. He just always seemed to know what was going on and never left anything to chance. Well, he was tipped off to this event just before it all went down and took immediate action. When he recognized the security breach, he knew that

121

he had to kill them all, and that is exactly what he did. Once Kazzar figured out that Saddam was on to him, he rallied together 20 to 30 of his closest allies in the government and they all piled into 10 Mercedes with about $40 million in cash. They headed straight to Iran to hide out. When Saddam realized that Kazzar was trying to escape, he sent out a bunch of helicopters to capture them. Once those helicopters caught up with Kazzar's motorcade, it was all over. Nobody ever heard from those guys again.

Although attempted coups and revolutions didn't happen very often, they certainly weren't out of the ordinary. That was what Iraq was like back then, very unstable with many different rival factions always trying to take power. Saddam was at the heart of it all and had very good reason to be paranoid. He murdered a lot of people to get to where he was and clearly wasn't about to give up his power without a fight. The fact that Saddam murdered people bothered me immensely. But what was I going to do? I saw a lot of my people get killed, and it really bothered me. I did what I had to do, though, to just get by. I never agreed with anything that guy did, but I had to do my job or maybe I would have been next. I never talked about it with him or anything like that; I just acted as normal as I could at the time. Usually, when I got home, I cried and cried, thinking about those people and about their families. It was very difficult, but something that I had to live with. I obviously knew that I had to get out of Iraq at that point, but the question was how.

In the meantime, as I got more seniority within the party I was able to flex my muscles a little bit. What I mean by this is that I was able to cash in a few more favors for friends and family from time to time. For instance, I might be able to get a guy out of prison, or maybe get somebody a passport out of the country—stuff like that. A lot of people would beg me to do stuff for them, though, and that got to be very difficult. They would come with pictures of their sons and beg me to help find them because they had disappeared. Once, a mother and father who I knew came to me and begged me to help get their son off death row. He was being held prisoner for some political reasons, and his parents were hysterical. I went to Saddam's office at the National Assembly and I told him the story, asking him to reconsider, but he said that the Revolutionary Command Council had already decided that the guy was guilty and he was to be executed. I felt terrible, but what was I to do? By nature I am a very giving person, so it was very difficult for me not to help them and others. Eventually, people realized that and took advantage of me. They knew that I had Saddam's ear and that he liked me. So I did what I could, but over time that got really old. It was difficult. I was a professional wrestler and just wanted to entertain people and give them something fun and positive in their lives; I didn't want to be a politician and be in a position to make decisions like that. I just wanted to wrestle and live a good life doing what I was doing. I could see that I was getting sucked

> I was a professional wrestler and just wanted to entertain people and give them something fun and positive in their lives; I didn't want to be a politician.

deeper and deeper into the spiderweb of Saddam's regime, and that scared me.

But there is one time I was able to help someone that I will never forget because the man was so grateful. One day my secretary told me that there was a young man there to see me. He said that he was a big fan of mine and that he would be honored if he could shake my hand, so I peeked out and saw that he looked like a nice kid and told my secretary to send him in. He came in and was shaking because he was so nervous to meet me. We started talking, and I asked him about his life and what he did for a living. He told me that he was very depressed because his wife was six months pregnant and he did not have a job. He said they were living in a one-bedroom apartment with no stove, no icebox, and no furniture, nothing. He told me that he was considering committing suicide, but he knew that he would be punished for it in the afterlife.

I wasn't sure if I could believe the guy or not because of all of the other people who were trying to take advantage of me and my generosity. So I sent for my driver and told him to go with the man back to his apartment to confirm what he had told me about his living arrangements. About two hours later he came back and said that it was all true, every bit of it. I genuinely felt bad for this guy and really wanted to do the right thing. I felt that his original intentions for seeing me were not to beg for money, and that made me want to help him.

I told him that I was going to help him and he just started to cry. I took him down and set him up with one of the government agencies that handled employment, and they got him a job that suited his skills. Then I told my driver to go back to the man's house and to order him a new icebox, stove, kitchen table, couch, bed, the whole works. I liked the guy, and I wanted to help him. He couldn't believe it. He just cried and cried and thanked me.

About two weeks later I got a call from the man I had helped, and he invited me over to his house for a lamb dinner with his wife. I agreed. When I got there I was really impressed to see how he had turned his life around. It made me feel really good about myself. He then told me that he wanted to name his baby after me, in my honor, but I told him that was not necessary. I then told him about an old Iraqi proverb that went something like, "They planted . . . so we could eat." This basically meant that our forefathers worked hard for us so that we, the next generation, could prosper. Then it would be our responsibility to do the same for the next generation. If everybody planted, then everybody could eat. It was very simple in definition, but very deep in meaning. He understood and vowed to do something good for someone else the same way I had done for him. That was one of the nicest things anybody has ever said to me; I was truly very touched.

> Even though I was using a lot of money to help people, it kept piling up. As I made more, ironically, it became increasingly more difficult to spend.

Even though I was using a lot of money to help people, it kept piling up. As I made more, ironically, it became increasingly more difficult to spend. The government took care of my house, my car, and most of my expenses. I couldn't transfer it out of the bank either, so I continued to spend it on nice things for others. Whether it was helping someone like that guy or buying my brother a new car, I just enjoyed giving—it was something that made me feel very good about myself.

15

Saddam's Rise to Power

EVENTUALLY SADDAM BECAME HEAD of the Baath Party. Ahmed Hassan al-Bakr was still the president, but he was old and clearly on his way out. Saddam was basically ruling from behind the scenes and doing whatever was necessary to eventually take over as the head of state. He was feared by the people and had the loyalty of most of the top brass in the government, particularly those in the military. He basically controlled the military. So at that point it wasn't *if* Saddam was going to take over, it was simply *when*.

Whenever anybody got too powerful or too popular, Saddam usually viewed them as a threat. One instance of this involved Hardan al-Tikriti, who was the minister of defense, deputy premier, and a former member of the Revolutionary Command Council. (He was one of the most beautiful men I had ever met in my life: he was so popular and had so much charisma, I just thought the world of him. He was truly the nicest guy you could ever meet.) He had been fired from his position by Saddam a few years earlier and told to get out of the country. So he wound up moving to Kuwait.

> [Saddam] was feared by the people and had the loyalty of most of the top brass in the government. . . . He basically controlled the military. So at that point it wasn't *if* Saddam was going to take over, it was simply *when*.

Several months later I had to go to Kuwait on official business to get some papers signed at the Iraqi Embassy there. When I got there, I saw the Iraqi ambassador and recognized him immediately as an old family friend. We shook hands, kissed, and started to visit. He then told me that he was on his way to see Hardan al-Tikriti, who was staying at a hotel in Kuwait City. He knew that I knew him and asked if I wanted to come along and have lunch with them. I told him I would love to but that I had a lot of official business to take care of and needed to get it done. So we said good-bye, and I went on my way.

The Iraqi ambassador met Hardan later that day, and just as he pulled up in front of Hardan's hotel to drop him off, all hell broke loose. A car pulled up alongside them and four guys jumped out with machine guns. They shot and killed Hardan al-Tikriti right there in the back seat of the car. My friend, the ambassador, was so traumatized by the incident that he couldn't function normally after that.

As the assassins were driving back to Baghdad, they got into a terrible car accident and three of them were killed. Ironically, the sole survivor was the brother of a prominent Iraqi governor from Samawa, Iraq, who was a friend of mine. The survivor was badly injured, however, and had to have both of his legs amputated below the knees. Believe it or not, the governor then asked me to escort his brother, the man who had killed my friend, to London to serve as his translator while he got fitted for prosthetic legs. I didn't want to do it, but I had to. The governor was a big RCC member, and if I didn't do this Saddam might get really mad at me, and I didn't know what might happen then.

So we flew to London, first class of course. The man had a big briefcase with him and asked me to carry it as a carry-on. I said, "Sure, no problem." Well, when we got to the security checkpoint in London the officer opened the briefcase, and in it was about $2 million in cash, all in crisp $100 U.S. bills. I couldn't believe my eyes. "What are you doing with all this money?" I asked. "Adnan, we are going to live off this money for as long as we are here, to eat, pay the hospital, hire security, and enjoy ourselves," he said. The security guy tried to make a fuss over it, so I had to explain to him who we were and what we were doing. I basically told him we were royalty and were there to do business. Once he realized all that money was coming into London and wasn't going back out, he let us right through.

We wound up staying in the penthouse of this really nice hotel while he got his legs fixed up. However, the entire time that I was there with this guy, I was disgusted with him. I wished that he would have died in that car accident, too. I knew that he had killed my friend, but there was nothing I could say or do about it. That was just the way it was. I am sure that he was following orders from the top, but it still hurt a great deal. So I tried to spend as much time as I could with the girlfriend I had in London from when I had lived there. I kept my car, a Jaguar, at her house, and sometimes I would go visit her on vacation and we would drive it all over Europe—it was wonderful. But that didn't last long, because the guy and I returned home after a few weeks. Ironically, he wound up dying about four months later due to complications from his leg operations. To tell you the truth, I was happy. I think it was God's way of making things right. I really do.

Back in Iraq, as Saddam got more and more powerful, he became more and more violent. After a few years of working for him I could see how paranoid and delusional he had become. I remember one time I decided that I wanted to see some of my old friends who I hadn't seen in years. There was one guy in particular who I really wanted to see and catch up with; his name was Khalid. He was an old high school friend of mine who I used to wrestle with. He had been very interested in politics and apparently got in way over his head. So when I couldn't get a hold of him, I told a couple of Saddam's security guys that I really wanted to see him. They kept giving me excuses as to his whereabouts, so finally I demanded to see him right away. I figured he was probably locked up somewhere and that perhaps I could help get him out.

After reluctantly agreeing, they took me in a car to this remote building outside of Baghdad. It was a one-story building, but it had several floors below ground. We got there and started to go down into the basement. It was really dark and dirty down there, and it really stunk, too. It was an awful place. We kept going down and down, and finally, when we got to the lowest level, a guy turned on the lights. I heard some running water at that point, like a faucet had been left on or something, and then I could see that the floor was all wet. Finally, they asked me if I was ready to see my friend, and I said, "Of course."

They opened a door, and a terrible odor hit me like a brick wall. Then I saw a body on a table that was just gruesome. It was all ripped apart and bloated. As I looked closer, I could see that there had been a garden hose shoved way up this poor man's ass, and water was coming out of his body from all over the place—his eyes, ears, mouth, all over. It was the most horrible thing I have ever seen in my entire life. They referred to this type of torture, by the way, as getting a "sprinkler." I am sure the body had been there for over a month; it was decomposing and the water was still running out of it. As I looked at his face I could see that it was indeed my friend Khalid. I couldn't believe my eyes—I had to get out of there.

> As Saddam got more and more powerful, he became more and more violent. After a few years of working for him I could see how paranoid and delusional he had become.

I ran up the long flight of stairs and got outside, where I threw up. I looked over at the security guys and asked them why anyone would do such a thing. They said that the Baath Party wanted to send a message to anybody who fought against them. You see, Khalid was originally a member of the Communist Party, but the party turned against the Baath Party for a period of time. When this happened, Khalid also turned against the Baath Party, so they had to take him out and send a clear message to anybody else who might want to do the same thing. There was no trial or anything like that; they had their own idea about how justice should be carried out. I was really scared. These guys didn't just expect loyalty; they demanded it.

I was sad for my friend, but I didn't feel like I was in danger personally. You see, I was very well respected and very well liked by both the common people as well as the government officials. I had come from a good family and was respected as a person and an athlete. Was I scared? Sure, but I didn't feel like I was going to be a target at that point. Yes, it was tough to see people get murdered, but I knew that as long as I kept my nose clean that I was going to be OK. It was just a unique time in Iraqi politics, and I guess I sort of tuned everything out in order to just focus on doing my job and not getting in the way. Even though I was a government official at the Ministry of Youth, I was not a member of the Baath Party. I was not political, and that gave me some level of security.

16

The Great Escape

TIME HAD FLOWN BY. After seven long years of living in Iraq, I could tell that the writing was on the wall as to my fate if I were to stay in Iraq. Eventually, I became too popular, and that was my undoing. Saddam had successfully used me to divert attention away from him and his rise to power, and in return I became very famous. Ultimately, however, Saddam did not like anybody more popular than himself.

Word got around that I was falling out of favor with him and that I was probably in danger of being assassinated. But because I was so beloved by the people, they wouldn't just shoot me or make me disappear. That would be too risky. Instead, they would stage an "accident" of some sort to make it look as though I had tragically passed away. That way Saddam wouldn't fall out of favor with the people for getting rid of me. It had happened before. Over the years many of the more popular ministers, politicians, and entertainers mysteriously died in accidents. In fact, just prior to this, Abdul al-Karim al-Shaikhli, the former foreign minister, was killed when he got into his car; it exploded when his driver turned the ignition. Again, he and Saddam were friends, but eventually he became too popular and had to go. I figured that my time was up as well and that I had better think about getting the hell out of Iraq before I, too, had a terrible "accident."

> I figured that my time was up as well and that I had better think about getting the hell out of Iraq before I, too, had a terrible "accident."

My brothers confirmed what I had been thinking all along and eventually told me that they loved me but would rather have me alive back in America than dead in Iraq. They knew that my time was up and that I had to get out while I still could. They were very afraid for my life. And I was now faced with the toughest decision of my life.

The first thing I did was go home and figure out exactly how much cash I had. I still had a couple million dollars in Iraqi dinars in the bank. But I couldn't touch it because I would have had to tell them that I was making a big withdrawal. I would have to fill out paperwork and make official requests, and by that time I could have been dead. There was no way around it. Everyone at the bank was a member of the Baath Party, so the party would have known what I was up to. They knew when my matches were and how much I typically deposited afterward.

So if I had a match, took money out, and then kept it, they would surely know and be suspicious. But I wasn't as concerned about the money; the most important thing for me at that point was making sure that Saddam didn't have an excuse to punish my family for something stupid long after I left. I knew that as long I kept my mouth shut about what I knew my family would be OK. Saddam had more important things to worry about at that point, and I think that as long as I was gone, that was good enough for him. He genuinely liked me and probably didn't want to see me dead, just gone.

As for my house and my car, I could not sell them either, so I was stuck. I was going to have to say good-bye to my shiny black Mercedes as well as my beautiful new house. I think my house was the toughest material thing to leave. I mean, it was incredible. If it were in America today, it would sell for several million dollars, no problem. Everything was top of the line, and they spared no expense to make it as opulent as possible: pure silk fabrics, Persian rugs, and mahogany wood, custom-built furniture. It was amazing.

It was so hard to leave it all behind, it really was. I had so many extravagant gifts that I had received from people, too, like gold watches, swords, and pistols. I just washed my hands of all of it. I knew that I could make more money back in America than my brothers ever could in Iraq, so I gave as much of it as I could to them and then started planning my escape. Luckily I had socked away some cash that I had converted to U.S. dollars on the black market during my first few years in Iraq. I had kept it hidden in my closet for a rainy day, and as far as I could tell it was pouring outside. I needed to get moving.

I had to be really careful not to tip anyone off that I was leaving. If anyone knew that I was going to move back to America at that point, it would have spread like wildfire and I surely wouldn't have been able to go. Saddam had increasingly made the borders much tighter over the years and had imposed much greater travel restrictions on the Iraqi people. Security was beefed up everywhere at that point because of increased tensions with neighboring Iran.

So after saying good-bye to my brothers and their families, I made the decision to go. I packed up a couple of suitcases with clothes and my most prized possessions and then loaded a carry-on bag with about $50,000 that I had saved. I went to work the next day and told my boss, who just happened to be Saddam's father-in-law, that I needed to go to London to take care of some official business for an upcoming match. Thank God he didn't press me too much about what I would be doing there, because I probably would have been busted on the spot. Luckily, he was busy and just signed my official papers without incident.

> Luckily I had socked away some cash that I had converted to U.S. dollars on the black market. . . . I had kept it hidden in my closet for a rainy day, and as far as I could tell it was pouring outside.

From there, I got my chauffeur and told him that I had some official business in Kuwait. Everything was going smoothly, but I was a little nervous about the border because my papers said that I was going to Europe. Fortunately the border guards all recognized me and didn't even ask to look at them. But just as we were about to leave, one of them asked me for an autograph. I was sweating and shivering I was so nervous. But I agreed, and with that we continued on to Kuwait City. I was almost home free. I just had to pray that the guards' reports did not make it back to Saddam's office until I was long gone.

When we pulled up to the Sheraton Hotel in Kuwait City that afternoon I instructed my driver to drop me off and then head back to Baghdad. Obviously I couldn't tell him what I was doing because he worked for the national security service and would have had to turn me in. I told him I was going to spend some time in Kuwait and that I wouldn't be needing his services. He reluctantly agreed and told me to call him when I needed a ride back. The next morning I booked myself on a one-way flight to London. I was free. It was a very sad flight, though, knowing that I would never have that life again. For seven glorious years I had been a hero, and then I had to walk away with almost nothing. But it was also an adventure knowing that I was going to be able to start over as a new person in a place that I had fallen in love with: America.

> For seven glorious years I had been a hero, and then I had to walk away with nothing. But it was also an adventure knowing that I was going to be able to start over as a new person in a place that I had fallen in love with: America.

17

America the Beautiful

WHEN **I** GOT TO **L**ONDON I met up with my girlfriend and we spent a few weeks relaxing in Spain. After that I got my Jaguar from her house and sold it. I then packed up some of my other personal belongings that I had kept in storage at her house and said good-bye. I flew to San Francisco, where I had made arrangements with a local promoter to begin wrestling as Chief Billy White Wolf again. Luckily, I still had my Indian costume in London, so I was good to go when I landed.

In San Francisco I basically had to start over, so I rented a furnished apartment. I then jumped back into the ring a few nights later. But to go from wrestling in front of several hundred thousand screaming fans to only several hundred screaming fans was quite an adjustment to say the least. Things were going to be a little quieter from then on, and that was just fine by me. In fact, it was kind of nice to finish a match and not have to worry about being shot.

Several weeks later I got a call from my brother back in Baghdad. He told me that the fans were asking and asking where I was and were wondering if I had been killed. He also told me that my picture had been on the front page of *al-Thawra*. The article basically said that I was AWOL and that unless I returned home immediately, I would lose my job at the Ministry of Youth and my title as the Arab Heavyweight Champion. I told my brother that what was done was done, and I was not ever going to come back. I told him I loved him, but that I had to make a new life for myself in America. To be honest, I figured that Saddam would be out of power in a few years, that he would be killed by either his enemies or his own people, and I would be able to return to Iraq at that point and resume my life there. I just couldn't imagine him staying in power for any length of time, but as we all know he did.

> Things were going to be a little quieter from then on, and that was just fine by me. In fact, it was kind of nice to finish a match and not have to worry about being shot.

My brother agreed and told me that if I came back I would definitely be killed. I told him to lie low for a while because

I did not want any trouble to come his way on account of me. My brothers were my only immediate family over there, and I was concerned for their safety. I just hoped and prayed that because I left behind all of my money, my car, and my house and kept my mouth shut that they would be left alone. Looking back, I think that Saddam figured banishment from Iraq and the loss of my fame and fortune coupled with the fact that I would not see my family again would probably be punishment enough for my leaving. After all, Saddam got exactly what he wanted in the end: he got rid of me. I had become a liability in his eyes and he was clearly on to much bigger things than having to worry about me. He was tightening his noose around the Iraqi people and his plan to use wrestling to unite the masses in order to divert attention away from his murderous regime had worked. I felt terrible, but for me it was do or die. I saw so many others who didn't go along with him get killed, and I did not want to die. I made the best of a bad situation, and when the time came to get out, that is exactly what I did.

After all, Saddam got exactly what he wanted in the end: he got rid of me.

Saddam forced out President al-Bakr shortly after that in 1979, and all hell broke loose from there. The regime eliminated an estimated seven thousand Iraqi Communists that same year and even expelled Ayatollah Khomeini, who had been exiled by the shah of Iran a few years earlier and was living in Najaf. At the age of just 42, Saddam held the positions of president, chairman of the Revolutionary Command

Council, secretary-general of the Baath Party, prime minister, and commander in chief. It was safe to say that he was firmly in charge.

The invasion of Iran came the next year, as did the massacre of the Kurdish people in the northern part of the country. I am glad that I got out when I did, because I probably would have had to fight in those wars. Come to think of it, I probably would have been killed either way. I was so relieved that I made it to America safely.

I wound up spending about eight months in San Francisco before returning to Hawaii the next year. When I was in Honolulu I decided to buy a condo. I figured it would always be there in case I ever lost all my money. (Luckily, I still have that condo—it was the best investment I ever made.)

In Hawaii, pro wrestling was nearly dead at that time. But it was a great place to live when you wanted to wrestle in Japan, Singapore, Australia, and New Zealand. The flights to those places weren't nearly as long from Honolulu as from the other states, so a lot of pro wrestlers were moving there for that very reason. You see, promoters were paying really well in the Far East at that time, and it was a good opportunity for me to do some more traveling. When I went to the Far East, I wrestled as both Chief Billy White Wolf and "the Sheikh." I was having success, too. In fact, I even served as the heavyweight champion of Australia for a pretty long stretch during the early eighties, and that was a lot of fun.

But my next big break in wrestling came one day while I was walking on Waikiki Beach in Hawaii. That day I met Verne Gagne, the legendary wrestling promoter, who was on vacation there after a trip to Japan. A friend of mine who I was with that day recognized him and introduced us. It's actually a pretty funny story. Verne had lost his luggage, so I loaned him some swimming trunks. We were both pretty big guys, so they fit him. He was grateful. After that we started talking and one thing led to another. I told him about my act, and he said that he had actually heard of me when I was an amateur wrestler at Oklahoma State. You see, Verne was an NCAA champ at the University of Minnesota back in the forties and had a soft spot for college wrestlers. Luckily for me, he told me to send him a tape of myself as the Sheikh. He said that he needed a new villain for his American Wrestling Association (AWA) promotion back in Minneapolis, and if everything looked good, I might be the guy.

I sent Verne my tape, and he called me immediately. "We need you here right away," he said. "Your tape was really good, and we have a spot for you right now if you can get here." I told him I couldn't come right away, but he insisted that I get there as soon as possible. About a month later I got to Minnesota—it was the dead of winter. Now, I had never been to Minnesota but had heard it could get pretty cold up there, but I had no idea how cold. When I stepped off the plane in a Hawaiian shirt and shorts, I just about died. I had never experienced such cold weather in my entire life; it must have been 20 degrees below zero that day. I couldn't believe it. I had no jacket, nothing. I thought to myself, "What in the hell have I gotten myself into?" A driver showed up to pick me up, and luckily he had an extra jacket for me. I asked him if it was always that cold, and he said, "No, it usually gets much colder during the winter months." I just about started to cry until he told me he was just kidding.

Managing in the AWA. Me and my entourage: the Mongolian Stomper, Boris Zuchoff, and the Barbarian. We're a fearsome gang.

The driver dropped me off, and I got settled in a hotel and began my new wrestling career in the Land of Ten Thousand Lakes. At first it was hard because I never wanted to leave my room. I didn't have a car, so it was difficult to get anywhere. I think I was getting depressed at that point. I had gone from living in a multimillion-dollar mansion to a tiny hotel room. I also missed my place back in Hawaii, where it was sunny and I could walk everywhere. But I needed to pull myself together so that I could move on. When I thought of it as the beginning of an entirely different era for myself, I got excited.

About a month later I got to Minnesota—it was the dead of winter. . . . When I stepped off the plane in a Hawaiian shirt and shorts, I just about died.

18

Stories of Life
on the Road

As the new decade of the eighties was ushered in, the American Wrestling Association was going strong, running events throughout the Midwest and into Canada. The biggest star of this era was Hulk Hogan, who quickly became a big fan favorite within the promotion. We could all tell that this guy was destined for stardom. After he was cast as Thunder Lips, alongside Sylvester Stallone, in the movie *Rocky III*, he became *the* guy in the business. He brought the AWA a lot of publicity, and I think we all benefited from that.

It was fun to work with people like him because the crowds got even more into it. Hogan was the ultimate babyface. And as the Sheikh I was a heel, as was said in the business.

As the hero, waving to my fans after a hard-fought victory in al-Shaab Stadium . . .

. . . and as the villain with menacing eyes.

It was a tough transition going from being a beloved baby-face to a hated bad guy. I played up the American stereotype of Arabs, though, and created a character who was perceived as an Arabian madman. I had a big sword, like Ali Baba's, and wore a traditional Middle Eastern robe and a turban. Sometimes I brought belly dancers with me to perform while I was doing television interviews. The fans really liked that. It was fun, but nothing like being in al-Shaab Stadium in front of hundreds of thousands of screaming fans who all wanted to embrace me.

> As the Sheikh I was a heel. . . . It was a tough transition going from being a beloved babyface to a hated bad guy.

Nonetheless, my career did take off in Minnesota, and over the next several years I became one of the promotion's top villains. I was working a lot with guys like the Crusher, Mad Dog Vachon, Baron Von Raschke, and Nick Bockwinkel. Bockwinkel had been the champion on and off for the better part of 10 years and was one of the most respected guys in the business. I will never forget one time when I was wrestling him for the AWA title belt and the crowd was loudly chanting "USA, USA" for him. Afterward, he told me he had never seen anything like that. I told him that after all those years he finally squared off against a better villain. We both had a good laugh after that. It was true though, I was a great villain, and I was very proud of that. It made our matches much better and a lot more fun because the crowd got into it so much more. Nick had hardly ever been cheered for in his career, but when I finally faced him the entire audience was in his corner. I guess he was the lesser of two evils.

For the first couple of years, I traveled extensively throughout the Midwest and Canada. The travel was brutal in those days; I was on the road constantly. I remember sometimes waking up in the morning and not knowing what city I was in. After a while it became a blur. But things got a whole lot better when Verne decided to get a corporate plane to fly to some of our matches. And there is one incident that happened on the plane that I will never forget.

The plane was a little eight seater nicknamed *Suicide One*. I was on board with seven other wrestlers, and we were on our way back to Minneapolis after a matchup in Winnipeg, Canada. It was January and about 30 degrees below zero outside. We were up in the air, and in the back of the plane was Adrian Adonis, this really flamboyant wrestler who was crazy. We were all tired from our matches and just relaxing when we heard Mad Dog ask the pilot if there was a bathroom on board. Obviously he knew that there was no bathroom on the plane, so I knew he was up to something.

Adrian said, "I am sorry guys, but I really gotta go." The pilot said he couldn't do an emergency landing for something like that, so Adrian would just have to sit for another hour or so until we got home. By then Adrian was beside himself, so he took out a plastic bag and proceeded to take a big dump in it right there in the back seat. The other guys ribbed him the entire time, but he didn't care, he was happy as hell. When he was done, the plane stunk like nothing I have ever smelled before. It was horrible, and we were trapped. I eventually had to stuff Kleenex up both of my nostrils just to breathe. I thought I was going to die—we all thought that.

Meanwhile, Mad Dog Vachon, who was sitting next to Adrian in the backseat, was so upset at how much it stunk that he reached over and just opened up the emergency exit door right then and there. It sounded like a bomb going off it was so loud. We all thought we were going to get sucked out, like in the movies, but luckily we were flying low enough that oxygen wasn't an issue. Mad Dog then threw the bag out the door and said, "How's that guys, better?" Meanwhile, the door was wide open and the plane was starting to go into a nosedive. The pilot pulled out of it, but the plane was bouncing all over the place at that point. And the engine was starting to sound funny, so we were getting really nervous. We had to get

> Mad Dog Vachon . . . was so upset at how much it stunk that he reached over and just opened up the emergency exit door right then and there. It sounded like a bomb going off it was so loud.

the door closed in order to equalize the pressure and reduce the wind drag, so we all took off our belts and tied them together in order to pull the door shut. We hooked it up and all of us pulled, but it wouldn't budge. By then the pilot was on the radio calling out, "Emergency landing! Emergency landing!" We all thought we were going to die. Guys were even praying—it was really intense. The plane was going up and down and up and down and pretty soon people were throwing up all over the place. It smelled even worse than before, it was awful.

Finally, we made an emergency landing and the pilot came back and started screaming at Mad Dog. He just looked up, smiled, and calmly said, "I needed some fresh air, it smelled bad." That was it. The pilot, who was irate at that point, said he refused to fly with Mad Dog ever again. In fact, he told him to take a bus home from there. We managed to calm the pilot down, though, and after we cleaned up the plane he agreed to take off again. This time Mad Dog had to sit up front with the pilot—where the pilot could keep his eye on Mad Dog to make sure that he behaved. Needless to say, that was the last time Mad Dog ever flew on the company plane. He was banned for life after that.

There are just so many hilarious incidents that I saw over the years, and I think that is what kept me sane. Another funny one happened around the same time as the airplane incident and involved legendary NFL Hall of Famer Leo Nomellini. The story actually begins way back in the early sixties, when I was wrestling in San Francisco. Leo had recently retired from playing with the San Francisco 49ers and was trying his hand at pro wrestling. I was assigned to do a tag-team match with him up in Portland, Oregon, so we drove up the coast together in his brand-new Thunderbird. I ended up falling asleep in the car, and when I woke up we were totally lost and about an hour off course up in the mountains near Crater Lake, Oregon. The radiator overheated and his new car started smoking. We were stuck in the middle of nowhere, it was dark, and there was nobody around, so I figured I might as well have some fun with the guy. I went and got my Chief Billy White

Wolf costume from my bag and put it on. He asked me what I was doing, so I told him that we were on a sacred Indian reservation and in real danger. I convinced him that we were being watched at that very moment and in all likelihood were probably going to be attacked with bows and arrows and might even get scalped. I was kidding of course, but he was just a rookie wrestler and had no idea.

> I convinced him that we were being watched at that very moment and in all likelihood were probably going to be attacked with bows and arrows and might even get scalped.

By then I was dancing around the car in my headdress, ringing my bells, and yelling into the mountains in Arabic that we were lost and meant the spirits no harm. Leo was beside himself at that point and was just hiding in the car, terrified. He was convinced that I was a real Indian chief and that I was out there doing a real sacred dance. Finally, a car came by and we got some water for the radiator so that we could get back on track. We hurried like hell and made it to our match that night with just minutes to spare, but Leo was still shaking in the ring because he was so scared about the Indian spirits. It was hilarious.

One night 20 years later I was wrestling as the Sheikh in Milwaukee, and Leo Nomellini showed up. He was there working for the local promoter doing some logistical stuff. He came over to me and introduced himself; he didn't recognize me. He asked me if I was new to the country, and I told him,

"Yes, I am." We started talking, and I asked him out of the blue if he ever knew a guy named Chief Billy White Wolf. "Yes," he said, all excited, and then he proceeded to tell me the entire story about how this brave Indian chief saved his life years ago up in the mountains of Oregon one night when his car broke down. Then he said, "Why? Do you know Chief Billy White Wolf?" I said, "As a matter of fact, I know him quite well . . . that's me." His jaw dropped to his knees. He couldn't believe his eyes, and we laughed for about 20 minutes.

Another funny thing happened to me one time when I was working over in Japan with a wrestling buddy of mine named Sammy. One night he picked up this beautiful girl at a bar and took her back to his hotel room. Well, a little while later, Sammy realized that the girl was actually a guy, so he went nuts and tried to smash a chair over the guy's head. The guy made it to the door, though, and started running down the hallway. It was 2:00 in the morning at that point and the guy was butt naked and screaming with a huge wrestler chasing after him. Finally, when they ran through the lobby and out onto the street, the hotel security called the police. Eventually they caught Sammy, handcuffed him, and threw him in jail. We had to go bail him out the next morning, and we laughed the whole time.

Some of the best times, though, came from jokes—or ribs, as they say in the biz—that we pulled on each other. One of the best ribs came on a flight from Winnipeg to Minneapolis with Ken Resnick, the ring announcer. There was a bunch of guys on the flight, and whenever you got a bunch of guys together, the ribs started flying. There was a really tough Japanese wrestler named "Mr. Saito" sleeping during the flight, so when his meal came the stewardess just put it on his tray for him to eat when he woke up. Well, one of the guys ate Saito's meal and left him with an empty plate. When Saito woke up he was really hungry, and when he realized what had happened he got really pissed. He looked around to see who did it, and all the guys pointed at Resnick, saying he was the culprit. Resnick, who was totally innocent, was just sitting there minding his own business. Saito then came over to him, and that is when all hell broke loose. Saito grabbed Resnick and started choking him until he finally escaped and ran up toward the cockpit. The passengers were now starting to freak out as these two idiots went at it up and down the aisle. Finally, the captain came out and threatened to throw them both in jail if they didn't get back to their seats. So they went back and sat down.

Later, at the airport in Minneapolis, Saito started chasing Resnick around again, this time outside into the parking lot, where it was about 20 degrees below zero. When the cops came running over to see what was going on, I told them that Saito and Resnick were professional wrestlers who had been hired as actors for a new hidden camera TV show that they were shooting in the airport that day. The cops bought it, and miraculously those two got off scot-free. Someone finally convinced Saito that Resnick wasn't guilty, and he eventually backed off. Saito was one guy you did not want to piss off, that was for sure.

Some ribs, however, simply went too far. I remember one in particular that happened when I was wrestling in Honolulu with Harold Sakata, who was later known as the villain Odd Job in the James Bond movies. Harold was a champion

155

weightlifter and karate expert, a really strong guy. One night during a live television show, he set up an exhibition in which he was going to break some thick wooden boards with his foot. The gimmick was that the boards were cooked in the oven beforehand so that they would break more easily. Another Japanese wrestler, "Mr. Fuji" (at least that's who I think it was, but I'm not sure to this day) switched the boards without Sakata knowing, replacing them with uncooked boards.

So the show started and the hosts introduced Sakata and told the viewers what he was going to do. A drum roll then started and Harold screamed "Banzai!" as he came running through the air to break the board. Whack! Nothing happened. He got up and did it again. Whack! Again, nothing happened. The hosts of the show asked him to try a third time, and that time he really kicked it hard. The only things that broke on that try, however, were several of his toes. We were all laughing but knew that he was hurt. They even had to carry him off the set, and he spent the next several weeks in a big cast. That was a rib that really got out of control. It could have cost him his career, but luckily he was OK. And he got into acting after that, so it all worked out in the end.

The dressing room was a place where interesting things went down, too. There were always two dressing rooms at the arenas: the babyface and the heel. The good guys got dressed in babyface and the villains in heel. I, of course, was always in the heel dressing room, and that made for some interesting observations. Not all the stories were funny, though. I remember one time there was a kid who worked for the AWA who served as a sort of gopher for us, bringing us our costumes and this and that. Well, this guy was very curious about the business and was always trying to snoop around in our stuff in the dressing room when we weren't around. He was a wannabe and stuck his nose where it didn't belong. He kept barging into our dressing room even though we had all asked him repeatedly not to bother us when we were getting ready for a match. Finally, Bobby "the Brain" Heenan really got after him and chewed him out in front of everybody. We thought that would do the trick, but sure enough, he came back a few nights later, and that is when Jerry Blackwell really let him have it. Jerry went crazy and head butted the guy several times, bloodying his nose and everything. He roughed him up pretty good; then he threw him in the shower and turned on the cold water just for good measure. It was really ugly. I tried to break it up a little bit when it got out of hand, but Jerry felt like the kid needed to learn a lesson. I guess the moral of the story is to never mess with a room full of villains.

The fans were always an adventure, too, especially for us villains. Sometimes they got out of control and really took things too far. Some of the fans really believed it was real, and those were the ones that you had to watch out for. I remember one time I was wrestling up in Winnipeg and a psycho fan attacked me from behind. I was walking back to the dressing room after my match, and he snuck up behind me and punched me in the back of the head. Then he jumped on my back and put my arm in a chicken wing (a type of arm lock), choking me really badly. I couldn't breathe or anything, it was awful. Luckily, some security guards saw me struggling and came over to help me out. They used a stun gun on him, and thankfully that did the trick. They then handcuffed the guy and brought him back to see me in the dressing room. They asked me if I wanted to press charges, but I told them to please leave us for a minute and wait outside the door so that I could talk to the guy alone. I wanted to scare the guy to teach him a lesson, and thought I would have some fun with him, too.

The guy sat down in a chair, and I brought out my big sword from my act and held it up for him to see. I screamed, "Where I come from we demand justice in our own way, and if you get caught doing something like that they chop your hands off!" I then motioned like I was going to swing my sword, and the guy just about went nuts. "No! No!" he screamed. He was terrified at that point, and I almost started to laugh. I then made him promise me that he would never do anything like that again. He got down on his hands and knees and begged me to forgive him. He even tried to kiss my boots, but I wouldn't let him. He said he would never do it again and apologized up and down. But I told him to get the hell out of there. Then, when I looked down at the chair where he had been sitting I realized that the poor bastard had pissed his pants. I started to laugh and told the security guards to let him go. I figured the humiliation of having to explain that to his buddies was probably punishment enough.

Groupie and wannabe fans were always fascinating to me, too. They were usually out in force at the arenas and at our hotels, always wanting to hang out with us. I remember one time when I was wrestling down in Australia with a group of Middle Eastern wrestlers. We were at a party together one night, and there was a tourist from Texas who just wouldn't leave us alone. He kept following us around and buying us drinks and was very persistent. Eventually, we started drinking arrack, an Asian liquor sort of like ouzo, but much stronger.

This guy couldn't take the hint that we didn't want him around, so we invited him over to have some fun with him.

He had a big cowboy hat on with cowboy boots and thought that he was a big, tough guy. So we started giving him shots of arrack. He was drinking and drinking and before long he was out like a light. When he almost fell off his chair, we knew he had had enough. But we knew that we couldn't just leave the guy there, so we picked him up and took him with us. He was staying at the same hotel as we were, so we carried him out to the car. When we finally got back to the hotel, we decided to have some more fun with the guy.

We stripped him down to nothing but his hat and boots and left him in the back seat of the rental car. Then we parked the car right in front of the hotel lobby and locked the doors. It was a five-star hotel, really nice, and we knew that this guy was going to be in for a surprise in the morning. The doorman finally came over to check out the car at about 2:00 in the morning and called the police. The cops came over and started knocking on the door. Eventually they pried the door open and realized that he was a hotel guest, so they took him up to his room and put him in his bed. The guy slept it off, but the next day the manager kicked him out of the hotel for good. That poor

159

SOB, but what can I say. That was the last time we ever saw the guy—he never bothered us again after that!

Another crazy side of the business is dealing with all the promoters. Every regional territory around the country had its own promoter who had his own set of rules and regulations. Some paid you on time and others made you sweat it out—that was just the nature of the business. I think every wrestler has had a run-in or two with a promoter over the course of his career, and I would have to say that the most talked about subject on all of those road trips we had together was promoters. In fact, everyone loved to talk about the art and challenge of successfully ribbing his promoter.

There was one promoter out in Portland who nobody could stand. He was really tight with his money and was just a real pain in the ass. One time myself, two other wrestlers, and that promoter took a road trip together after a match. We were headed to another match in Eugene, Oregon. We cracked open a couple cases of beer and hit the road in his brand-new car. It was late, and before long we had to pull over to relieve ourselves on the side of the road. One of the guys got a crazy idea to piss in the gas tank, just to get back at the promoter for all the money he had shortchanged him during his career. From then on, every time we stopped, one of us would piss in the tank while the other guys shielded him from the promoter's view. It helped that it was dark out and he couldn't see a thing. I think we must have filled the entire gas tank up, we stopped so much. Finally, the car started smoking and flat-out died on the side of the road. The promoter was really upset that his new car quit like that, and he couldn't figure out what the hell had happened. So a wrecker came and towed us all the way to

Eugene. We all just tried not to laugh out loud; it was terrible. I think that every wrestler in the state of Oregon heard about that story over the years; it was like an urban myth after a while. Life on the road was something else.

Another story involving a promoter happened at Chicago's Rosemont Horizon Arena. I was doing a tag-team match with King Kong Brody against Mad Dog Vachon and Verne Gagne. It was a sold-out match, and there were a lot of screaming fans there. Verne, who was probably well into his fifties at the time, was still the champ, and the fans loved him. Brody and I were the villains, meanwhile, and the crowd was totally against us, it was great. Gagne, in addition to being the world champion, was also the promoter. So basically he was our boss, and it was always tough to wrestle against him because we didn't want to hurt the guy who signed our paychecks. The match got underway, and I wound up on top of Verne. I was supposed to jump on his back as part of a move, but he stood up in the middle of it and I came down on him really hard, breaking four of his ribs. I could hear them crack, it was so loud. That was typical Verne, though, never wanting to "sell" a move for anybody else. He was legendary for stuff like that, and that was why guys hated to wrestle him. After that move, though, he was really upset and in a lot of pain. He could hardly move. He leaned over to me and mumbled, "I am really hurt; don't touch me. I can't breathe; just get me over to the corner." So he crawled over and tagged up with Mad Dog, telling him to finish up and to get him the hell out of there. Mad Dog came in and finished us off so we could get Verne to a hospital.

Afterward, the crowd was really pissed at me, and they were letting me know it. As I was walking back to the dressing room,

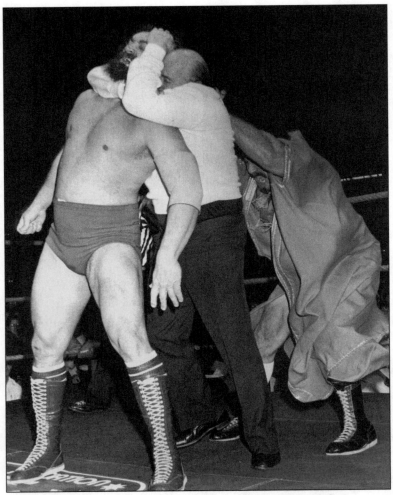

Hitting Verne Gagne from behind as he applies his vaunted Gagne Sleeper Hold on my partner, King Kong Brody.

two drunk fans jumped me and were determined to try to kill me. Brody came running over to help me, but not before I took some good shots to the head. Brody, who is just huge, smacked one of them in the head, and I think he broke the guy's neck. The other guy grabbed me and wouldn't let go of me until the security guards pried him off. It was really scary. After it calmed down, the security guards brought the guy back to us to talk to him and let us have a few words with him. They used to let us handle a lot of this stuff back in those days rather than get the police involved. Brody and I threatened to whack him around a little bit, and the guy finally broke down and begged us to let him go. He got down on his knees and told us that he was a married man and promised never to bother us again. We knew that we couldn't touch the guy, otherwise we would get sued in court, so we gave him a good scare and just let him go.

> After it calmed down, the security guards brought the guy back to us to talk to him and let us have a few words with him. They used to let us handle a lot of this stuff back in those days rather than get the police involved.

Verne came back a few hours later all bandaged up and was really pissed off. I got chewed out pretty good and had to just take it. Any other guy would have been fired, but I was his top heel and he needed me. One thing about Verne, if he could make money on you, your job was safe. I just apologized and bit my tongue as he let me have it. What was so funny, though, was that later that night and into the next day I must have gotten about a hundred phone calls from all the other wrestlers in the promotion congratulating me for what I had done to old Verne. Even though I had always been a villain, on that day, I was finally the biggest hero of them all, at least in the eyes of my peers.

One of my favorite people to travel with was Eddie Sharkey, an old-school wrestler who was also a legendary trainer up in Minnesota. Eddie was full of stories and that is what made him so likeable. He could get a group of guys together and just start telling tall tales, it was wonderful. He told us about what life was like on the road back in the early days of the business, when the action spilled out into the crowds—where it was unpredictable and downright dangerous.

YOU KNOW, THE SIXTIES were the toughest time in pro wrestling, no doubt about it. We didn't have any police protection back then like they do now. There were no barriers up either, so we had to form a V and fight our way through the crowd to get in and out of the ring. It was tough; fans would be all over you. Remember, they still thought it was all real back then, so if you were a villain, they hated you, and some of them really wanted to hurt you. Guys would get stabbed, hell, sometimes we would come out of a match and a guy's car would be on fire. These people didn't mess around.

So we had a lot of big guys who were good amateur wrestlers with us back in those days, but a lot of them didn't know how to throw a punch. I mean, you were not going to get some big drunk in a hammerlock out there and take him down, because the crowd would kill ya before you had the chance. I was an escort, a puncher, as we were known, for guys to get into and out of the ring. Sure, if I had to crack a few heads out there to get by, then that is what I did. The key was to just sucker punch the biggest one and then keep walking, never running, because that would panic the crowd into a riot. There were no lawsuits back then either, so we could do whatever the hell we wanted to. Nowadays, jeez, these idiots would own my house and car; it is an entirely different era.

Anyway, one time in Denver, after a match, we were walking back to the dressing room and a drunk fan attacked my partner, Harley Race. I looked over and saw that this guy had him in a death grip around the waist. He wouldn't let go either. On top of that, there was a woman smacking him over the head with her high-heeled shoe. It was nuts. So I ran over and kicked the guy in the head as hard as I could. Well, he didn't let go, so I reached over to stick my finger in his eye, only it went right into an empty socket. Harley, who had just gotten his finger bitten off, had already pulled this poor SOB's eye out! We got the hell out of there fast. So Harley was full of blood at that point and we had to go over to the hospital to have his finger put back on. Well, sure enough, there was the other guy, who came in to have his eye fixed up. They both got patched up, and we all laughed about it later. Of course, we could never go back to Denver after that, but hey, that was wrestling in the sixties, it was a crazy time.

After an alleged incident with the boss, Verne Gagne, Eddie decided to hang up his tights and try his hand at becoming a promoter and trainer. That story as Eddie tells it is pretty hilarious, too.

ONE TIME I GOT PRETTY TICKED at Verne about the way I felt he was treating my wife, who was also a pro wrestler, so I headed up to the sixth floor of the old Dyckman Hotel, where the AWA's offices were, and I wanted to make a statement. So I pulled out my gun and blew the s*** out of the place, something like 14 rounds I think. It was like a James Bond movie. You know, back in the sixties, almost every wrestler carried a gun. It was a totally different time. Verne wasn't there or anything, I just wanted to make a statement I suppose. I don't know if I would have actually shot him if he had been there—maybe just one bullet in the leg or something, nothing serious. Then I walked out of there real cool, right through the lobby. Afterward, there were no hard feelings, Verne and I made up and he even booked me on his cards after that. The bottom line for me was that I was ready to get out at that point, I wasn't enjoying it like I used to.

Being a promoter was a tough job, though, and one time in Wisconsin, Eddie tells us, his temper got the best of him, and it cost him big-time.

I AM VERY LOYAL TO MY GUYS, and this promoter shorted us a hundred bucks, so I punched him. Then, just to be cute, I broke a beer bottle over his head, which was a big mistake. If I had just behaved myself, I would have gotten a simple assault charge, but instead I got a felony. Well, at the trial I tried to show the judge that that particular brand of beer bottle wasn't very thick and couldn't possibly cause very much damage. So I took one out of my bag and smashed it over my own head right there in court. Well, he wasn't impressed, so I got six months at the Hennepin County Workhouse. I was still able to go to work everyday, but I had to sleep in jail. I even had to pay like 37 bucks a day just to stay there on top of everything else; that was tough. I learned my lesson after that one.

As a trainer, Eddie found his calling. He discovered everybody from the Road Warriors to Rick Rude to Jesse Ventura, and was truly one of the best in the business. He says he still misses the good ol' days.

THERE WERE SO MANY CHARACTERS back in the day. They were all half nuts, or they wouldn't be in this business. We've been accused of a lot of things, but never of being dull people. Say what you want, but we had so much fun in those days, we were laughing all the time. You know, I used to own a house in south Minneapolis, and Harley Race lived with me. Harley was so tough, our fights were classics. It was never a question of if we'd win or lose, it was how quickly we could knock the other guys out. Anyway, there was this wrestler, Jose "Bad Man" Quintero, who was crazier than a s***house rat. Well, he came to town one time and had no place to stay, so I rented him Harley's closet, at half price, of course. Well, one time that I will never forget Harley came home from a long road trip, and he went to hang up his coat in his closet, and when he opened up the door he nearly died of a heart attack when he saw this weird-looking dude with beady little eyes sitting in there staring back at him. Oh, those were the days.

Eddie is a classic; he's really old school. There were just so many great stories, and those memories are like treasures to me now. It is a unique fraternity being a professional wrestler, and yes, I am proud of it. I think back about all of those stories from over the years and just have to smile.

The American Wrestling Association family photo.

19

Down for the Count

By **THE MIDEIGHTIES** pro wrestling's popularity was growing like crazy, not only in the United States but also abroad. I began performing more and more around the world. And, in addition to competing in Japan and Australia, I even got an opportunity to go back and wrestle in the Middle East. Pro wrestling had really grown over there, and a promoter from Lebanon begged me to come back and perform for him in a match in Kuwait. At first I was afraid to go back because I didn't know if Saddam would send somebody to take me out. He had spies all over the world and could easily get me if he wanted to. But after talking to my brothers, I realized that if Saddam was going to do something to me, he would have done it by then. He had much more important things to worry about than me, including the war with Iran, so I decided to go.

Being back was wonderful. Several of my friends drove down for the match, and it was so great to see them. But they brought some sad news, too. They told me that Saddam was ruining the country and that the future was bleak. So many people had died in the war over the past several years, and it was very sad. In fact, when it was all said and done, it was estimated that there were nearly 1 million casualties, including two hundred fifty thousand Iraqis, in the eight-year war. Saddam had used chemical weapons against both the Iranians and the Kurds—he was out of control. It was unbelievable. I was really glad that I had gotten out when I did.

As for the match in Kuwait, everything went off without a hitch. I didn't end up having any scares with Saddam. But my partner Eddie Sharkey, my favorite storyteller, had a little one of his own. At first Eddie and I got delayed at the airport because he gave the customs official his visa card instead of his visa passport. But once we got that mess straightened out we went to the hotel. I was exhausted and just wanted to get some sleep. We got settled in our rooms, and later that night Eddie knocked on my door. "What is it, Eddie?" I yelled. "I need to move to a different room, right away," he said. So I got up, put on some clothes, and went down to his room with him. "Well?" I asked. "What is the problem?" "Look out the window," he said. So I opened the curtain and there, pointed right smack dab at his room, were two Russian tank turrets. You see, our hotel was right next to the Russian Embassy, and they were on high alert. I looked at Eddie, smiled, and said, "No problem, Eddie. We can get you a new room." It was nothing like the scares I used to have when I would fly guys into Iraq and have to worry about Saddam shooting them if they accidentally hurt me, but it was pretty scary for Eddie.

When we got back to the States I continued to wrestle around the country, gaining more and more popularity as I went. Even though the character that I portrayed was a villain, by that time people understood that it was just an act. When I was on the street or at a restaurant, people used to come up to me all the time to tell me that they enjoyed watching me. I always felt honored when somebody told me that they liked my character and that they wanted to shake my hand. I was very good at what I did, and I am proud of that. They said they enjoyed me as an entertainer, as an athlete, and as an interview subject.

> I opened the curtain and there, pointed right smack dab at his room, were two Russian tank turrets.

A big part of pro wrestling is doing interviews, and I was very good in front of the camera. Early on in my career I used to wave a big saber and, often, I had belly dancers around me, so it was very visual and interesting to watch. People wanted to tune in to hear what sort of outlandish things I was going to say, and then they wanted to see if I could follow up on my predictions in the ring the next week. Wrestling was all about selling your image and keeping your story lines going for as long as possible. I think it represents every walk of life in society and whether it is to a good guy or a bad guy, everybody can relate to somebody. That is what keeps the fans coming back for more.

In the ring during my days with the American Wrestling Association. The referee is Brad Rheingans, a fellow wrestler who is only acting as the referee.

About a year later I injured my knee really badly in a match. I knew something was wrong right away, and I knew I was in trouble. Until then I had been lucky and avoided any major injuries over my career, but I made up for all of that right then. I had some surgeries on my knee and then went through rehabilitation for a long time after that. I was able to come back for a while, but eventually it forced me to pretty much retire from active wrestling. My doctor basically told me that if I kept wrestling there was a good chance I might never be able to walk on it again. So that was it.

It was a big blow to me, however, knowing that I could no longer do what I loved to do. As a wrestler, my body took such a pounding over the years, and the damage to it had been building up for a long time. I was also worried about being able to make a living for myself. I didn't have a lot to fall back on. Sure, I had a master's degree, but I never worked in the mainstream job market. I had always been a professional wrestler; it was who I was.

Because I had no intentions of retiring at that point, I decided to become a manager. Managers were a part of the acts but typically didn't get into the ring to wrestle. They stood on the side of the ropes, talked trash, and tried to interfere with the referee in order to help their guys win. It was all good fun. As for me, my mobility was severely limited after my injury, but I wanted to stick with it. I could still get into the ring; I just couldn't do too many acrobatic moves. But to sell the idea of me transforming into a manager, I had to come up with a retirement angle for the fans to follow along with. So I suffered a tragic "career-ending" neck injury at the hands of Ken Patera, a former U.S. Olympic weight lifter and World's Strongest Man competitor. The fans bought it.

All I needed after that was a gimmick, so I called Jerry Blackwell, as well as Patera, and pitched them on the idea of making a new tag-team act with me serving as their manager. They agreed. For the gig they changed their personas to match my own, each wearing traditional Middle Eastern robes and playing the parts of newly converted Arab warriors, nicknamed "the Sheikhs." It was a lot of fun, and it actually proved to be quite successful. We, of course, were heels, and the crowds loved to hate us. Jerry, who was close to 500 pounds, took the name

"Ayatollah Blackwell" and developed a very loyal following. The guy was huge. Wrestling under his own name, Patera, meanwhile, was also quite famous and had a really mean, tough demeanor. We got a lot of heat and fit together very well.

> The idea was to come in, beat the good guys on their own turf, talk trash, and then lose to them in dramatic fashion. After that, we got out of Dodge.

We toured all over the country with different promotions and got to be one of the hottest acts around. Promoters wanted to bring us in because they knew we would draw huge crowds for them. Sometimes we would go into a new territory and stay for anywhere between one night and several weeks. The idea was to come in, beat the good guys on their own turf, talk trash, and then lose to them in dramatic fashion. After that, we got out of Dodge. That way it was always new and fresh, with a lot of dramatic plot lines, just like a good soap opera.

To me, wrestling was like art imitating life in many ways. People just love to root for their heroes and boo at their nemeses. We played the bad-guy role very well and really got the crowd to hate us—that was our job. And when we did a good job, we got paid more, because it meant that more people were either coming out to see us or tuning in on their televisions at home.

As the Sheikhs, Patera, Blackwell, and I eventually won the AWA Tag Team Title by defeating the High Flyers, Greg

Gagne and Jim Brunzell. We kept a stronghold on the title belts for the next year or so, and every time Patera and Blackwell were in danger of getting beat, I would somehow interfere with the referee and wind up saving the day. It was a riot. We seemed destined for a long title reign at that point, but an incident that happened outside of the ring quickly changed everything.

The night of April 6, 1984, in Waukesha, Wisconsin, is an evening I will never forget. We were all staying at a hotel after a match. Patera was hungry, so he walked next door to grab a burger at McDonald's. When he got there, however, he was allegedly denied service. So he got upset and tossed a huge rock through the window. He then casually walked back to his hotel room. Shortly thereafter, a couple of police officers showed up to question him. His roommate, Mr. Saito, answered the door. The officers asked to speak to Patera, but Mr. Saito played dumb. The officers then tried to get into the room, and that is when all hell broke loose. The grappler resisted arrest, and in the ensuing melee, which spilled into the hallway, a couple of officers were injured. Other policemen joined in from there and subdued the two, ultimately taking them to jail. I was staying in the hotel room next door and saw the whole thing go down. I couldn't believe it. They were later found guilty of battery, and as a result, Patera wound up spending more than a year in the slammer.

I continued to manage after that with Jerry. Jerry was a real character. He ate like a pig and really never tried to lose any weight as far as I could tell. And, despite the fact that he ate tons of junk food, he was very sensitive about being so overweight. Traveling with him was always an adventure. We stayed in the same room together, and it was insane living with him.

He would sit up all night watching TV, eating chips, and drinking Coke, until he fell asleep when the sun came up. Meanwhile, I would be up by 5:00 in the morning and out the door for my morning workout. I had to baby-sit him wherever we went, and it was really tough.

I remember one time we were on the road and I had rented us a new Lincoln. We took off from a match one night, and while we were on our way to the next city, I stopped at a grocery store in this small town for us to grab some food. Jerry, of course, took his sweet time in there buying bags and bags of chips and soda. I got done early and waited for him out in the car in the parking lot. I waited and waited until finally I started driving around the parking lot to see if I could find him. I didn't know what the heck had happened to him. Eventually, I saw him sitting in the front seat of another Lincoln in the parking lot. He obviously got confused and was sitting in there eating chips and waiting for me to show up. As I pulled up to honk at him, this sweet elderly couple walked up and found big Jerry sitting in their car. They started motioning him to please get out of their car, but Jerry thought they were ridiculing him, so he lashed out and screamed at them. They got scared and went back inside the store to get the manager.

I was laughing my head off at that point. The manager then came out with some security guards and tried to explain to Jerry that he was in the wrong car, but Jerry wouldn't listen to them. He had the windows rolled up and was determined not to move an inch. Finally, I pulled up in my car in front of him and beeped my horn, winking at him. He was just furious. I could see him swearing and throwing his chips in the car, just mad as hell—he had to gather up all his stuff and take the walk of shame over to my car. It was hilarious. The old couple couldn't believe their eyes when he got out of the car. He just looked over at them and sneered as he slowly came over to our car. That was Jerry. He let me have it after that one, but all I could do was laugh.

Being a manager was both good and bad. I was happy to still be in the business that I loved, but saddened by the fact that I wasn't earning nearly what I had as an active wrestler. I ended up working as an independent contractor and was bouncing around between different promoters trying to get as many jobs as I could. It was a slow time for me, and I was struggling to get my career back on track. I wanted to get back into the game, but with a bad knee I was limited. It was tough.

The business was changing by that time, too. Vince McMahon, the owner/promoter of the powerful World Wrestling Federation (WWF), had been raiding the talent in the AWA for years. Everybody from Hulk Hogan to Jesse Ventura had left Gagne to join McMahon in New York. He had a lot of money and lured a lot of guys away over the years. McMahon's philosophy on entertainment was very different from that of the small-time promoters, such as Gagne.

> McMahon's philosophy was based more on televising short, action-packed, made-for-TV vignettes. . . . Gagne, meanwhile, was an old-school guy who believed in athleticism over entertainment.

Managing Russian wrestler Boris Zuchoff in the AWA before I became General Adnan.

While McMahon was focusing on the entertainment side of the business, Gagne was hanging on to the more traditional athletic approach. McMahon's philosophy was based more on televising short, action-packed, made-for-TV vignettes, complete with extremely risqué and oftentimes very sexual story lines with beautiful women. Gagne, meanwhile, was an old-school guy who believed in athleticism over entertainment. He was of the opinion that his wrestlers' matches should last much longer and feature back and forth selling, maneuvering, and strategizing to tell the story. McMahon's style, on the other hand, was all about big-time entertainment. After all, he was the one who broke the code of silence. Pro wrestling had always considered itself a "sport" (as Gagne preferred it). And as a sport it was sanctioned by various local athletic commissions. These commissions were set up in certain states to regulate the ethics and rules of various sports, particularly boxing because of the gambling it involved. They then imposed commissions on sports, such as pro wrestling, in order to verify the sport's claims of validity and authenticity. (They also regulated such things as worker and fan safety and protected the states from frivolous lawsuits.) But the ruse was up in the mid-eighties when McMahon decided that he no longer wanted to pay hefty fees to the commissions and publicly declared that pro wrestling was no longer a sport but a form of entertainment, showbiz.

> The writing was on the wall as to the future of the industry. And sadly, in 1991 the AWA conceded and closed it doors forever.

181

In laymen's terms, he had just explained in detail how the magician pulls the rabbit out of his hat. Deep down, sure, we all sort of knew, but the mystery and drama was what kept us coming back for more. So with McMahon changing the face of wrestling and with all the dollars he was throwing around, the writing was on the wall as to the future of the industry. And sadly, in 1991 the AWA conceded and closed it doors forever. The whole thing was really unfortunate because then my future was even more uncertain.

And by then it wasn't just me that I had to worry about. I had settled down and gotten married. My lovely wife Kathy and I had purchased a home in the Twin Cities suburb of Minnetonka and were ready to start a family. The only thing we needed was for me to catch a big break in my career. Incredibly, thanks to the stupidity and greed of Saddam Hussein in the summer of 1990, that is exactly what I got.

20

General Adnan
Takes Charge

IN AUGUST 1990 SADDAM INVADED neighboring
Kuwait. Stories of looting and pillaging ran wild as his elite
Republican Guard forces took over the country and laid claim
to its rich oil empire. Shortly thereafter the United States got
involved, and that fall coalition forces came to the aid of Kuwait
in what was later termed Operation Desert Storm. Saddam suddenly became a household name in America, and stories of his
brutality quickly made him enemy number one.

I remember getting a call one day from Vince McMahon
as all of this was going on. He said that he had a great idea
that he wanted to run by me. He knew that I was Iraqi and
he knew that I had worked with Saddam, so he had come up

with a gimmick that would bring me back into the action. I listened very intently—McMahon was a billionaire, and if he wanted you to perform for him, you did it. His idea was to turn this other wrestler, "Sergeant Slaughter" (Bob Remus), a real over-the-top U.S. Army drill sergeant, into a villain. The angle was that Slaughter, this die-hard American military hero, was so upset over the U.S. invasion of Iraq that he decided to turn against his own country. Being an Iraqi, I would serve as his manager under the name "General Adnan," a character that looked and acted just like Saddam. It would appear as though I had brainwashed Slaughter and convinced him to become a traitor to his own country. Pro wrestling was all a big soap opera, and this was going to be one of the biggest and boldest plotlines they had ever come up with. Whenever you start mixing sports and entertainment with real-life issues, such as war, you are going to get a strong reaction from people. The reaction we would get, however, would be stronger than anything in pro wrestling history.

> The reaction we would get, however, would be stronger than anything in pro wrestling history.

I agreed to do it. I knew that I was setting myself up for a lot of heat, but I wanted to get back to work and I needed the money. I figured that this was just the booster shot that my career needed, and if I was going to have to take a big risk doing it, then so be it. I was going to use Vince McMahon, and Vince McMahon was going to use me. To be honest, I really had no other options at that point.

With that I got to work creating a costume. It took a couple of weeks to put it all together—the army boots, the uniform, the beret, the sunglasses, the gun, the belt, the Iraqi flag, the medals, the whole nine yards—it was really something. It came out looking just like Saddam's military uniform. Then I grew a thick mustache to make the whole thing look perfect. From there, I headed out to see Vince in New York to show him how it looked. By then, Saddam was on the news every day and everybody in the world knew exactly what he looked like.

When I got out there, I put the whole outfit on and then came out to see what Hogan thought. He was taking a nap at the time, so I snuck up behind him and said to him in this deep Arabic voice that I was Saddam Hussein and that I was going to take him hostage. He jumped up and just about s*** his pants. He couldn't believe it. "Oh my God, that is incredible," he screamed. "Adnan, is that you?" So I said, "What do you see?" And he said, "I see Saddam Hussein, brother. I see a million bucks. You are going to make nothing but money on this brother, nothing but money." Hulk then ran out and grabbed Vince. When Vince saw me, he too couldn't believe his eyes. I almost thought he was going to have a heart attack right there. He said that the outfit was perfect and that the gimmick was going to be big . . . really big. It was all set.

From there, I got together with Slaughter and we went over our game plan. He too was in a situation where he needed the work. He had been very popular during the eighties but had fallen out of favor with McMahon, so for him to get this opportunity was big. He knew the risks, but, like me, was willing

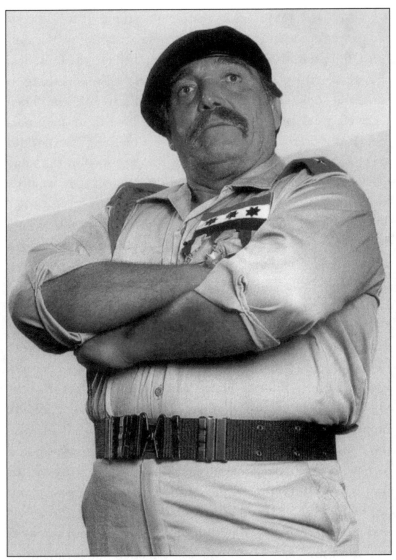

"General Adnan" staring down the competition.

to go for one last hurrah in the limelight, and hopefully one more big payday.

I got Slaughter outfitted with an Iraqi military uniform just like mine. I even had a pair of Arabian-style boots made with a curled-up toe that were supposedly a gift from Saddam himself. He looked great, and with that we hit the road. I don't think either of us had any idea just how strong the reaction was going to be over our act, though. We knew that the Gulf War was going on, and we knew that we had to be sensitive to that, but we also had to be way over the top in order to sell the gimmick. The heat we were about to get was unlike anything I had ever known.

As we would come out for the matches, the crowds booed us mercilessly. Before the matches started, I used to give a big speech in the ring, denouncing the U.S. military and explaining how I was going to convert more U.S. soldiers to sympathize with Iraq. A lot of times I spoke in Arabic to make it feel more authentic. I led people to believe that I too was under the spell of Saddam and that I was taking over the minds of even the toughest American soldiers. I made it very personal and very political on purpose; I wanted to get a reaction out of the crowd, and that is exactly what I got.

Then, when the match started, I stood ringside, giving Slaughter advice and always trying to interfere with the other guy when the ref wasn't looking. It was all part of our act. Usually, at the end, we would both get in the ring and beat the hell out of our opponent to win the match in a really dirty manner. We got more heat that way, meaning we got the crowd to hate us even more, and that was the point, because then they were interested in us, and paid attention to us, and wanted us

Sitting ringside and barking out orders to Sergeant Slaughter.

to get beat. It was a soap opera, and everybody quickly began to ask the big question: Who was going to finally beat these jerks?

What was tough about the act was the fact that I had to sell the idea that I completely condemned the U.S. invasion of Iraq and the Gulf War. That was obviously not a very popular position to take at the time, but I knew that to make the character credible, I had to really put myself out there. I was very against Iraq invading Kuwait; it was wrong. When the United States went over there to liberate Kuwait, I was all for it. I knew that things were going to get tough for me after that, as well as for all Arab Americans, but that was just the nature of the situation. Portraying this character was tough to do, but it was something I did as part of my act, in order to feed my family. Aside from all of the political implications and the crazy people who sent us death threats, the act was actually really fun to do. To be able to control a crowd like that and have them eating out of my hand was exciting. And, for me, it was neat to see that I could be just as influential as a bad guy as I had been as a good guy over in Iraq.

Before long we were selling out arenas from coast to coast. We got so hot, it was unbelievable. I think even to this day, it might be the hottest thing in the history of pro wrestling. It created such a sense of nationalism, I couldn't believe it. The fans would chant "USA, USA, USA." It was really something. And just like when I wrestled in Iraq, sometimes I couldn't even hear myself think in the ring, it was so loud. And they sold more American flags at the concession stands during those matches than anyone could ever believe. People were waving two at a time. I am sure McMahon made a fortune on those, too.

I remember performing at the Spectrum in Philadelphia one time in front of a packed house, and the head of security there told me he was going to need a tank to get me out of there alive. He said it was seriously dangerous and that I should be very cautious at all times so that I didn't get attacked by some nut. Just getting into the ring was like running the gauntlet. There were people everywhere, and they wanted to reach out and grab me as I walked by. The crowd wanted to tear me apart, and it was very frightening to tell you the truth. We had to have dozens of security guards escort us wherever we went.

> I think even to this day, it might be the hottest thing in the history of pro wrestling. It created such a sense of nationalism, I couldn't believe it. The fans would chant "USA, USA, USA."

That night I wound up getting in the ring against "Hacksaw" Jim Dugan, who was really popular at the time. I jumped in and started kicking him with my big army boots and was really letting him have it. I was taunting the crowd and they were screaming at me so loudly that my head hurt. Finally, as the crowd was chanting, "USA, USA," he got me turned around and let me have it. He body slammed me and then whacked me over the head with a big two-by-four that he carried around with him as part of his act. I was out for the count, and the crowd erupted with cheers. The passion and emotion of the crowd were surreal. And getting out of there was an adventure in itself. The security had to cover me up and huddle around me to get me back to the dressing room. It was actually like that wherever we went—from California to New York, we were the hottest thing going.

I enjoyed getting back into the ring. It was nice because I knew that even though I would usually be in there for just a few minutes, nothing was going to happen to me. The guys who we competed against knew going in that I was absolutely off-limits. Believe me, if somebody reinjured my knee so that I couldn't perform anymore, McMahon would have fired them on the spot. We were hot, and nobody wanted to jinx it. And even though some guys might have been jealous of our success, they knew that they were all going to make money off of us by virtue of the industry getting more exposure as a whole. In fact, our act was so controversial that we were even being featured on the national news programs.

During our heyday, Vince used to call me all the time. Sometimes he would be in his private jet, other times at his office in New York. Because we were so hot at that time, he wanted to keep me posted on just about everything. It was fun to be in that position again, in a position of power. I found that power is like a drug; I craved it. I hadn't felt that powerful since my days of wrestling at al-Shaab Stadium in Baghdad. And Vince fed that feeling. He told me he had never seen anybody get more heat than me in all his years in the business. That was a pretty big compliment coming from him, because he is a very sharp guy and understands marketing better than just about everybody. He knew that the more heat a wrestler got, the more popular he was. Popularity didn't necessarily mean that the character was liked; in fact, I was despised, but that was the point. The more hated I was, the more liked the other guys who wrestled us were. The crowds were always very polarized that way.

As a result of our success, all of the other wrestlers in McMahon's stable wanted a piece of us in the ring. They were begging Vince to let them wrestle us. They knew that they would get huge television numbers competing against us, and in turn, they would make more money. You see, pro wrestlers work on commission, so to speak, making a percentage of ticket revenues, television revenues for pay-per-view events, and merchandising revenue. So the hotter a wrestler was, the more money he made. For a while, we were *it* in the world of professional wrestling.

21

Feeling the Heat

AFTER ABOUT A YEAR OF DOING OUR ACT it got to be a grind. We were going really hard, and it was getting tough. We had to wear disguises and change our identities when we were outside anywhere, and it was a very scary time for both of us. We both got death threats, and there were times when I was genuinely scared for my family, not just myself. I know that at one point Slaughter was really terrified for his life and strongly considered quitting the act. Someone apparently threatened to burn his house down and even harm his children. I think the FBI finally had to come out to protect him. I felt really bad for him.

Eventually, I received a call from someone at the U.S. Department of State in Washington, D.C. He told me that what I was doing was insane and that while he couldn't legally

Carrying the Iraqi flag into the ring alongside Sergeant Slaughter.

stop me from doing what I was doing, he strongly recommended
that I put away my Iraqi flag immediately. He said that
Americans were dying in Iraq and that I was being insensitive
to what was going on. Pointing out that the pro wrestling crowd
was unlike any other in the sports/entertainment world, he said
that I was clearly on my own when it came to protecting myself.

And he told me flat out that if I got killed by some nut, it would not be the government's fault for not protecting me. Basically he told me that if somebody got mad enough, or if someone's father or son got killed over there, then that person might try to do the same to me. He then said it would be tough for me to get a jury to convict someone who tried to beat me up or kill me after what I was doing. In fact, he said they would probably give the nut who did it a medal instead of a prison term, and he would be looked at like some sort of heroic martyr.

By that point I was pretty scared, so I immediately took the Iraqi flag out of my act and tried to tone it down a bit. I even considered calling the whole thing off myself, but I had to weigh it against the money I was making with the act. I talked to my wife about it, and she said that she trusted me to make the right decision. So I stuck it out. Really though, I was very conflicted. I mean there I was, a proud Iraqi torn over the war back home. I knew that many of my nephews and cousins were being forced to fight in Saddam's Republican Guard. They were being bombed every day, and if they deserted, they would be shot. Seeing the bombs explode and watching my hometown burning right before my eyes on television was just terrifying. To know that my brothers and their families were over there and going through all of that was very tough. I couldn't get in touch with them either because the phones had been knocked out during the war. So I didn't know if they were alive or dead. All I could do was sit back and wait. On the other hand, I was an American citizen with an American wife and American kids. It was one hell of a way to make a living, I suppose. The bottom line was that we were making a lot of money, so it didn't matter. I knew that this might be my last opportunity

195

to make some good money, and knew that I had to see it through to the end—whenever that would be.

Wanting to keep our act fresh, Slaughter and I later agreed to add some new blood to the mix. So, at the request of Vince McMahon, we brought in another wrestler by the name of Kosrow Vaziri, who had been well known as the "Iron Sheikh." For our gimmick, however, he would become "General Mustafa," an Iraqi sympathizer now serving as one of my top generals in the Republican Guard. Together we would be known as the "Triangle of Terror." This added a little bit more drama to our act and gave us more story lines to pursue.

Together we would be known as the "Triangle of Terror."

There was never a dull moment with Kosrow. In fact, his story is as fascinating as he is. An outstanding amateur wrestler in Iran, he came over to America on a real leap of faith. There was a guy in Minnesota by the name of Alan Rice, who was a former Olympic Greco-Roman wrestler. Rice knew that the Iranians were outstanding wrestlers, so he recruited their top Olympians to come overseas to train at the University of Minnesota. He fed and housed them in exchange for their teaching his kids about international wrestling. Before long a whole bunch of Iranian wrestlers were lining up to come over and see America.

One night Rice got a call from a security official at the Minneapolis airport telling him that there was a foreign guy there who couldn't speak English but knew two words: *Alan* and *Rice*. That guy turned out to be Kosrow Vaziri, who had spent every dime he had to buy a ticket to come to America.

The Triangle of Terror: General Mustafa (Kosrow Vaziri), Sergeant Slaughter (Bob Remus), and General Adnan.

He didn't know a soul, but he knew of Rice, so he literally just started yelling his name at the Minneapolis airport. Rice came down, picked him up, and put him up at his home. Later on, Rice, who had wrestled with Verne Gagne at the University of Minnesota back in the forties, introduced Kosrow to Gagne, and that is how Kosrow got into professional wrestling as the Iron Sheik. It is a great story of how the American dream can work.

Kosrow really struggled to learn English over the years, but I got along with him pretty well because I could speak Iranian. One funny incident that happened because of his struggles with English came years later when I was General Adnan and

197

we were wrestling together as the Triangle of Terror. Kosrow had a gimmick in which he was supposed to talk about U.S. General Norman Schwarzkopf in one of his interviews as part of his schtick. Well, he couldn't pronounce Norman Schwarzkopf to save his life, so he said the next best thing instead: Arnold Schwarzenegger. Everybody just about died. I had to come to his rescue and bail him out, and the guys never let him live that one down.

> He couldn't pronounce Norman Schwarzkopf to save his life, so he said the next best thing instead: Arnold Schwarzenegger.

As the Triangle of Terror we continued wrestling to packed arenas around the country and eventually got our big break at Royal Rumble 1991, when Slaughter was given the green light to beat "the Ultimate Warrior" for the WWF World Heavyweight Title. That really pissed the fans off but good. From there, we beat Hulk Hogan in a highly publicized television match. I wound up jumping in the ring and beating him up pretty good, it was great. The crowd wanted to ring our necks, which was exactly what we wanted because the stage was then set for the rematch in Los Angeles at the pay-per-view spectacle *Wrestlemania VII*.

Wrestlemania VII was unbelievable. They promoted it like nothing I have ever seen. It was huge. In fact, it got so out of control that the feds got involved and actually forced McMahon to change the location of the event from an outdoor stadium to an indoor arena, because of all the death threats we were getting.

Here we are as champs.

Slaughter and Hogan wound up going at it in the main event for more than 20 minutes (a normal match lasts 15 minutes), and the crowd ate it up. The match went back and forth with a lot of good action. I was on the sidelines for the most part, but was able to interfere with the referee at just the right times to really get under his skin. I eventually gave Sarge a chair

Wrestlemania VII *in Los Angeles between Sergeant Slaughter and Hulk Hogan.*

and he whacked Hogan over the head with it, bloodying his face really good. Hogan actually cut himself, which is known as "blading" in the business, but it looked really good with all of the sweat coming off his face. Slaughter then locked his camel clutch finishing move on him for the kill, but Hogan dramatically powered out at the last second. Slaughter then shoved Hogan into the corner, grabbed an Iraqi flag, and tried to smother him. Hogan countered by kicking him in the groin, and then Slaughter was down for the count. Hogan celebrated by holding up his WWF Heavyweight Championship belt along with an American flag.

Sure, it was an over-the-top patriotic ending, but the fans really enjoyed it, and that is what it was all about. More importantly, however, the event generated a record $145 million in sales, making it one of the top-grossing events in the history of sports entertainment.

22

Stepping Out of the Limelight

AFTER *WRESTLEMANIA* WE KEPT THE ACT GOING for a few more months. We knew that the gimmick was losing its appeal, though, because the war itself was winding down. So it was decided that our big finale would take place at another pay-per-view spectacle called *SummerSlam*. Held at Madison Square Garden, the event was another blockbuster. We sold the place out, and the intensity in there was amazing. The fans were all over us, and it got pretty scary at times. New York is always an exciting place to perform, but this time it was out of control.

Slaughter, Mustafa, and I went out with a bang, losing a tag-team match to Hulk Hogan and the Ultimate Warrior. The

Holding Hulk Hogan while General Mustafa kicks him at SummerSlam *1991 in Madison Square Garden.*

story was that after the match Hogan and the Ultimate Warrior "unbrainwashed" Slaughter and he became a born-again American patriot. We staged it so that he and I got into a big fight in the ring after the match and I slapped him hard across the face. He then attacked me and announced that he had fired me right then and there. He got down on his knees and apologized to the American people for his actions and begged for their forgiveness on camera. The crowd loved it. Again, the show brought in really big numbers, and McMahon was very happy.

With that, we were done. That is how it is in this business: here today and gone tomorrow. By the time our act was over, the Gulf War was over and sadly, so was my career in the WWF. I asked McMahon if I could continue with the company after that, perhaps working as an agent, but he said that there were no opportunities for me at that time. I was really pissed after that, because I went through a lot during that time and sacrificed a great deal for him. I made him a lot of money and didn't feel like I was treated right when it was all said and done. But hey, it's a business, and we all knew that going in.

> That is how it is in this business: here today and gone tomorrow. By the time our act was over, the Gulf War was over and sadly, so was my career in the WWF.

As for Slaughter, his story is pretty interesting. He had actually left the WWF to go out on his own a few years before we started our act. He had been selling his own GI Joe–type action figures, and there was a falling out between him and McMahon over that. But Vince knew that Slaughter was the only guy on the planet who could pull off the act with me. So he had to eat a little crow and ask him to come back. What's funny about that, though, is that McMahon got the last laugh by turning Slaughter into a villain. Slaughter had always been a beloved army hero and there he was as the most hated guy in the building. Me, I was used to that. I had been a villain for years in America, and that was all I knew. But Slaughter really had a tough time with it, and I think McMahon enjoyed that. When it was all said and done, Slaughter's reputation was tarnished, no question. But McMahon knew that Slaughter was going to make the best money of his life doing this gimmick and therefore wouldn't care that he had to sell his soul in the process. McMahon was very shrewd in that way, and he never forgot if somebody tried to screw him. He might not get revenge right then and there, but he would definitely get it when the time was right. He got Slaughter back all right and even made millions of dollars in the process.

To tell you the truth, when it was over I was actually pretty relieved. I was making great money during that time, but I couldn't wait for it to be over. It was very stressful for me and my family. I just needed to get away from it all and get back to my normal life for a while. I had been gone, traveling almost nonstop during that year and a half, and I just missed my family. Plus, I wasn't going to miss being hated so badly and having to always worry about my personal safety. A person can only take so much of that, even if it is all part of his act. I just wanted to go back to being a husband and a dad for a while.

After taking some much-needed time off, I did some independent shows around the Midwest. I had gained a lot of name recognition over the previous couple of years, and I wanted to parlay that into more work while I still could. I had a couple of nice gigs, including one with the American Wrestling

Sergeant Slaughter: the hated villain.

Federation, where I continued to manage many wrestlers, including Boris Zukhov, King Kong Brody, the Barbarian, and the Mongolian Stomper. I later even started my own promotion along with Ken Patera called the World All-Star Wrestling Alliance. But it all came to an end after only a year or so.

> Looking back and reflecting on the entire saga is something I do a lot these days. I got a lot of criticism for creating General Adnan, but I would probably do it all over again in a minute.

Looking back and reflecting on the entire saga is something I do a lot these days. I got a lot of criticism for creating General Adnan, but I would probably do it all over again in a minute. It was definitely a controversial thing for me to do, and I knew that I was capitalizing on the events that were going on back in my home country. In the end though, I decided to do it in the most respectful way possible so that it would be nothing more than entertainment. I needed to make a living, and the opportunity presented itself, so I took it. I have no regrets.

Somebody once asked me if I thought Saddam ever knew that I was impersonating him, and if so, would he be upset? You know, I am not sure, but I would think that because we had a relationship before, he probably would have gotten a kick out of it. But who knows? He had huge satellite antennas at his palaces to pick up TV signals from around the world, so maybe he was watching and booing me along with everybody else. Plus, he had spies working for him all over the world telling him everything that was being said about him. The guy was so paranoid. So he probably knew. I think he would have taken it as a huge compliment that I was taking all of this heat just trying to imitate him. He probably thought I was defending him and his actions. Well, if he did, he was dead wrong. He can think whatever he wants, but I did it for one reason and

The real me in a recent photo.

209

one reason only: because Vince McMahon promised me a lot of money. Period.

As for me, for the last several years I have continued to live in both the Twin Cities and Hawaii with my wife and four children. I am 65 years old now, and believe it or not, I still perform at small, independent shows around the Midwest on the weekends. It is in my blood, and I just can't let go. It's not al-Shaab Stadium, or even Madison Square Garden, but it's a living. I also manage a few young guys these days and see the twinkle in their eyes in anticipation of what it would be like to make it to the big time. I now live vicariously through them and enjoy it a great deal.

I also am very involved in both the Lions and Elks clubs, where I try to do as much charity work around the community as I can. I also occasionally promote my own independent wrestling shows in conjunction with those organizations to raise money for various charities. A lot of former pro wrestlers live in the area, and we all help each other out that way. The fans love it when we get out there, and it keeps us young. My benefits have helped raise funds for local youth sports teams, and we even did a really big show to raise money for the victims of September 11, which was something that I was very proud of.

I am also very proud of my Iraqi heritage and proud of where I came from. In fact, I have spoken a lot at local schools and at other benevolent organizations over the years to tell them about my situation back home. I want people to understand that Iraqis are good people and that for the most part they too were happy to get rid of Saddam. When I tell young people my story, they listen. I think they can relate to me because

I was a professional wrestler, and I am just a normal guy. I think I have made a difference with them. I am proud of the fact that I have been able to leave people with a good impression of both Iraqis and Muslims. It is all about the next generation, and I hope they will see things differently than the current one does.

You know, I want to do whatever I can to do my part here in America. I have even offered to act as an interpreter for the government or to take on any other tasks that might help bring terrorists to justice. I see the world differently after 9-11 and pray for peace every day. I just hope that positive changes will come soon from my friends and family back home.

I am also very proud of my Iraqi heritage and proud of where I came from.

As for my family here in America, sure, it has been trying at times for all of us. I think it has been difficult for my family to be a part of all of this, no question. They see me hurting and they too hurt. I am truly blessed, though, to have such a loving and supportive family. I have four children: Kahtan (16), Khalil (14), Cassidy (11), and Sophie (7). They are all very smart and all are involved in various activities, from sports to church. They are just very sweet kids, and Kathy is a wonderful mother. She works, and she raises four kids. It is pretty remarkable how she does it all. I am very proud of her; she is a great woman. I am also proud to be a Muslim, and I am proud to say that my wife, Kathy, is a Catholic. My children have the luxury of having both cultures, and hopefully that will only make their lives even richer in the future.

23

My Two Cents on the State of the State

As FOR THE FUTURE OF IRAQ, I am optimistic. I think that I have a unique perspective on the current situation there as well as what it might take to one day achieve peace in the Middle East. Being an Arab American is not always the easiest thing to be in this post–9-11 world. Sure, I experienced some racism after those tragic events; I think all Arab Americans did, and many still do. That is just the reality of living in America and having to deal with the fact that the terrorists who did those horrible things that day were all Muslims. They do not represent me or anybody that I know, though, and they certainly do not represent the religion of Islam either. Islam literally means "peace," and what the terrorists did to all of those innocent people certainly had nothing to do with peace and is beyond anything I could ever comprehend.

Islam

literally

means

"peace."

A lot of people ask me to articulate to them why relations are strained between America and the Middle East. I don't profess to be an expert on foreign affairs by any stretch, but I have insight from living in both places for many years. And from talking to others about the situation, I have a pretty good pulse on what the attitudes and feelings are amongst both Muslims living in the Arab world and Arab Americans living here in America. Arab Americans think that American foreign policy has not been trusted very well in the Arab world. They also think that when 9-11 took place everything changed. After the United States invaded Afghanistan and then Iraq, many Muslims felt that the United States was getting in too deep. Most of the Arab world felt badly for the United States after 9-11. But many felt that after the United States decided to establish more of a presence in the Arab world that they were doing so more for spreading Western views and Western culture than for fighting terrorism. They also felt that oil was a big factor, too.

There are roughly a billion and a half Muslims around the world today with the vast majority living in the Middle East. I think that many Arab Muslims feel threatened that the United States is going to try to spread their ideologies about Christianity into Muslim life, and that scares them. They feel that over time the United States may invade other countries and spread Christianity to those places as well. Again, these are not my opinions; they are just observations that I have made from speaking to many people over the years. I want to articulate my thoughts as well as those of others who can't speak English and try to help Americans better understand the situation from the other side of the fence. My main goal in writing this book is to help promote peace. That is my sole intent.

As for the U.S. invasion of Iraq in 2003, I support the United States; I think all Iraqis are grateful that Saddam is now out of power. Many will argue over the way that it was done, but few will argue with the outcome. Still, the outlook in Iraq as of right now is grim. When the U.S.-led coalition forces didn't find weapons of mass destruction, I think that made it worse. Now, with the pending occupation, it is really a mess.

Iraq has been at war in one way or another for nearly the entire time I have been gone and living in America. . . . Enough is enough. The Iraqi people want peace, and they deserve peace.

It is important to realize that the people of Iraq have been suppressed for a long time. Iraq has been at war in one way or another for nearly the entire time I have been gone and living in America. It all started in the late seventies with Iran and then continued with the Kurdish uprising, followed by Desert Storm, and now Operation Iraqi Freedom. It has been nonstop violence for these people for more than 25 years. Enough is enough. The Iraqi people want peace, and they deserve peace.

I think most Iraqis also understand that they must sacrifice now in order to have a stable, peaceful democracy in the future. Hopefully, in 10 years, Iraq will have a bustling economy and a whole new sense of optimism. Wouldn't it be great if one day Americans could go to Baghdad on a vacation to see the ancient sites? Wouldn't it be great if one day children in Iraq could grow up with the same opportunities that kids in America have, like going to college and getting a good job? I dream of this and realize that we are closer to it than ever before. Sure, there is a long, long way to go, but getting rid of Saddam and his torturous regime was the first step toward accomplishing this goal.

> Wouldn't it be great if one day children in Iraq could grow up with the same opportunities that kids in America have, like going to college and getting a good job?

As far as the immediate future of the country is concerned, I am very saddened. With all of the suicide bombings, the kidnappings, and the beheadings—the despair—I pray every day that things will get better. It is an ongoing situation that is very troubling. On one hand I am so anxious for the United States to withdraw and leave Iraq so that the country can begin again as a new democracy. Then, on the other hand, I am terrified for the day that the United States leaves because then the rival factions and insurgents may start a civil war. If that happens there will be so much bloodshed. I fear that a civil war in the Middle East would one day result in a worldwide disaster. Oil markets would crash, and

God only knows how many would die—millions. It would be horrific. I just hope and pray that nobody ever gets a nuclear bomb over there; it would be a catastrophe like none ever before seen.

You know, I think Americans got their first real taste of terrorism on September 11, 2001, and that made everybody here stand up and really take notice. We can never forget that day, and we must all work toward achieving peace in our own ways to make sure it never happens again. My hope is that we can all make a difference in the world and try to make our country the best, safest place it can be for future generations. If we all do our part, then the sky is the limit.

24

A Lifetime of Memories and a Few Big Dreams

I **HAVE HAD A VERY BLESSED LIFE** and feel as though I have truly lived the American dream. While I am not a rich man, I have riches beyond my wildest dreams when it comes to having a wonderful family and friends. It has been an amazing journey, and I am very proud of my achievements. I love this country and am so grateful to have had the opportunity to live here and to raise my family here.

Today, Iraq is liberated, the tyrannical dictator Saddam is gone, and my self-imposed silence has finally been lifted. For 25 years I have not been able to go back to Iraq because I was afraid of what Saddam or his two evil sons, Odai and Qusai, might have done to me. I was afraid they would make an example out of me, or worse yet, take it out on my family. So I left and never looked back. Now, with all of them gone, I can't wait to go home. That is my dream. I miss my family, and I miss my country. Sure, I am an American now and my family is American, but to be able to come full circle would make me so happy. I want to visit my Iraqi relatives in Baghdad, and I want to be able to bring them here to see my American family. I speak often with two of my brothers who live in Baghdad, Kamil and Jalil, about what is happening over there. They are pessimistic about the short term but optimistic about the long term. With all the uncertainty, I pray for them every day.

> I have had a very blessed life and feel as though I have truly lived the American dream.

But what I really want is to visit them. To be able to return to Iraq in the next year or so and see my family would be a wish come true. My brothers are getting old now, into their seventies, and I desperately want to see them again before it is too late. I am anxious to go back and celebrate how far we have all come. And I know that there are so many Iraqi Americans who feel the same way that I do. They came to America in search of a better life, like all immigrants have done through the years, and now they want to go back to visit so that they can further the cause. Now, thanks to the United States, they can start the long road to recovery. It will be a wonderful new chapter in Iraqi history and I can't wait to see it come to life.

When the United States finally leaves, Iraq will most certainly rise up and return to her former glory. I really do feel that the vast majority of Iraqis want to see peace and they want to see their country become one of the greatest democracies in the world. The Iraqis want the same things that Americans want: peace, safety, jobs, and a better life for themselves and their children.

I also think we are all anxious for Saddam's much-publicized trial to start and to hear what he has to say. Frankly, I am surprised that the United States took him alive. They took out his two murderous sons, but I think they wanted to show the world that one of the more important aspects of democracy is the right to a fair trial. I don't know how in the world you could ever have a fair trial with this guy, though. I mean he is the most infamous dictator on the planet, and everybody knows that. It should be very interesting to see how he spins his own story. You know, Saddam thought he was above everybody else. He figured that there was no way that the United States would ever double-cross him back when he invaded Kuwait in the early nineties. He had worked very closely with the United States for many years during the war with Iran and didn't think they would even bat an eye at him annexing the tiny little country of Kuwait. Well, as we all know, he was dead wrong. People don't realize just how much the CIA built up Saddam during

> The Iraqis want the same things that Americans want: peace, safety, jobs, and a better life for themselves and their children.

that time and how much they gave him in order to beat the Iranians. Then, when he got too powerful, they came back to crush him.

I, like most Iraqis, just want justice. Saddam deserves whatever he gets, that is for sure. I would like retribution, too. I mean, I wonder where he hid all of those billions of dollars he stole from the Iraqi people. I think if they got that back and used it for good causes, then that would be wonderful. But I still have the fear that he could get off. I can't imagine what would happen if he were to be found innocent of war crimes and of defying the United Nations; that would be incredibly difficult for most Iraqis to take. But Saddam killed so many people over his 30-year reign that I can't imagine that he wouldn't be found guilty. Still, you never know—especially if he is allowed to use his "own" money to buy a top defense team. One thing is for sure, if he is publicly executed there will be dancing in the streets of Baghdad. It would be one of the biggest spectacles in history. It wouldn't surprise me one bit if they had a firing squad take him out at al-Shaab Stadium. The whole thing is very upsetting—it is so difficult to see how this man single-handedly destroyed our country. But I suppose we'll just have to wait and see what happens at the trial. I will be watching, like everybody else, and eagerly awaiting the outcome.

> The whole thing is very upsetting—it is so difficult to see how this man single-handedly destroyed our country.